① STRING BOILING RECIPE

Ingredients

One set of greasy strings
One pan suitable for boiling
One square of tin foil suitable for wrapping and baking
One fork suitable for poking holes in the tin foil

1. Wind the strings up into a circle small enough to fit into the pan you're using.

2. Boil in regular tap water for 15 minutes.

3. Carefully remove and dry with a clean towel (not paper towels).

4. Wrap in foil and perforate with the fork to let air circulate.

5. Preheat oven to lowest temperature possible, around 220°F.

6. Dry in oven for 15 min.

7. Remove and allow to cool.

8. Reinstall the strings for that bright "almost new" sound.

② EYE CONTACT

In any band situation, eye contact is the cure for most train wrecks. But it can also cause train wrecks if you're not careful when you use it. If you're in charge for giving a cue (telling the band when to move to the next section), then it's better to avoid making eye contact with anyone until about two bars before the change. Then all it takes is a couple of raised eyebrows and wide open eyeballs, and everyone will get the message.

With practice, everyone can learn to rely on your cues, and transitions can be made smoothly. Sometimes you have a situation when you have to relay a cue to the rest of the band. In that case, you stare down the "cue-er" and don't make eye contact with anyone else until you receive the cue.

Timing is everything. Say you're playing music with two-bar phrases. The best cue is given two bars before the transition happens. If a cue happens in the middle of a two-bar phrase, then a wreck is about to happen... Are we one bar away or is it coming three bars from now? By the time you can answer, half the band has already switched while the other half has got that "deer in the headlights" look...

3 TAKE THE 5TH (FOR IMPROV)

As a bass soloist, you have two strikes against you before you ever start soloing:

1. You've learned to hear and play music from the root up.

2. The register of your instrument keeps it lower in the harmonic spectrum.

This makes it difficult for the bass to sound like it's playing "over" the music in a melodic fashion. One way to get your ideas to sound above the harmony is to start your ideas from the 5th.

If you're playing over a Cmaj7, play as if you were playing a Gmaj7.

Just playing a triad on G gets you the 7th and the 9th, which already sounds "above" the harmony. Even if you play that triad as low as you can on the instrument, it still sounds above the harmony. It's important to keep the sense of separation between melody and harmony by avoiding roots at the beginning and end of any ideas you play. By thinking of Gmaj7, you'll avoid the 4th (a.k.a. the root, C) and maintain that separation.

Here's an example of centering some solo ideas around the 5th.

The basic G, D, and B in the first bar create the sound of the 5th, 9th, and 7th while the C, A, and F in the third bar do the same. This results in a solo that sounds more like it's "above" the harmony.

This is the same progression for you to work on:

4 SO MANY MELODIES...

As a bassist, you're used to moving the music along from underneath. The music won't go anywhere unless you do. It's complelely different when you're the melody instrument. The music goes on underneath whether you play anything or not. Melodies can speed up, slow down, start late, or start early, and the accompaniment goes on, regardless. The more melodies you learn to play, the more you'll get a sense of the independence the melodic instrument has from the accompaniment. And the more you learn to interpret* melodies, the more you'll be able to personalize and interpret your own ideas.

*Interpret...If you just play what's written on the page, you're not really communicating anything. Melodies need to be interpreted. Make subtle changes in phrasing, coloration, decoration, whatever you can add to make the melody more personal and human.

5 SPEAKERS UP

If you find that the bass is too boomy for the room, try raising your speaker cabinets off the floor about a foot. When they're on the floor, there's a "coupling" that goes on that makes the floor vibrate and reinforce the bass sound throughout the stage. Raising the speakers off the floor "uncouples" them and gives you a tighter bass sound. Also, it puts the speakers closer to your torso and ear so you can turn down and still hear yourself well.

Bass frequencies require huge surfaces before they reflect. This is why you might find that your volume setting on stage in a huge concert hall is actually less than the setting you use in a tiny rehearsal room. The walls in a rehearsal room are too small to reflect the bass frequencies, so you have to compensate with more volume.

6 DRUM MACHINE DON'TS

If you practice with full-blown, perfectly mixed drum machine grooves, then you'll create a dependency on hearing those full-blown, perfectly mixed drums whenever you play. You want the band to be able to rely on you for a sense of time and groove, so you should learn to rely on hearing less when you practice.

The most reliable instrument in a drummer's kit is the hi-hat. Bass drums, cymbals, snares, and crashes can be all over the place. but the one thing that's consistent is the hi-hat. Usually it's not the easiest thing to hear, but you can hear it in between the beats. Put the hi-hat on the "ands" of grooves. If a groove is "quarter note at 120," put the hi-hat at 120 but make it on the offbeat. This forces you to come up with the downbeats and a sense of time while listening for the in-between consistency of the hi-hat. The band can then rely on you for a sense of time without you needing the full-blown, perfectly mixed drum mix to play to.

3 Here's a full-blown groove.

4 Here's the same tempo for you to practice with, but with the hi-hat only ($\downarrow$ = 106).

Back in the day—O.K. I'm showing my age here, but back when I was learning to play—we didn't have drum machines. All I had was a Franz electric metronome with a loud "in-your- face" smack when the beater hit the side of the box. I did some modifications by covering the inside of the metronome with duct tape to dull the "clack" sound it made and occasionally put a pillow over it to simulate the softer presence that a hi-hat sound usually has in the mix.

7 THE ONE-CHORUS SOLO

A big challenge for bass soloists comes when it's time to end a solo. Why? Because we have to seamlessly switch roles from soloing to accompanying without stopping. This transition period is often the most critical, since a great solo can lose its momentum and impact if the end and transition is not handled confidently. If you wait too long before ending your solo and making the transition, then the rest of the band is usually not ready to come in. If you finish too early, then there's not much the band can do except twiddle their thumbs until the beginning of the next section.

Practice solos that only last one chorus, and really target the transition. Since you're usually higher on the neck, definitely work on anticipating when it's time to work your way back down to a register where you can comfortably resume your role. If you execute the end of your solo and make the transition confidently with the right timing, you'll immediately be rewarded by a tremendous standing ovation and a showering of gifts and possibly undergarments. Or at least you'll avoid a musical train wreck.

8 SET UP ON THE HI-HAT SIDE

It may sound kind of obvious, but some people don't realize the importance of setting up on the hi-hat side of the drum kit. The other side is where you'll hear more of the less-consistent instruments like the ride cymbal, crashes, and toms. As well as having a better chance of hearing the snare, you'll want to set up on the side of the most consistent instrument in the drum kit. (See #6.)

9 IMAGINARY FINGERING

You can actually get a lot of work done learning the fingerboard away from the bass. Imagine a finger per fret, and use your thumb to contact the finger that corresponds to the note you're fretting, imagining string changes as necessary. Then start playing. Try starting off with "Twinkle Twinkle Little Star." How about "Happy Birthday"? If you're listening to the radio, imagine the tune in C, starting with your second finger, and play along. If you find a note outside that initial four-fret area, straighten your thumb out to the side to remind yourself that you're stretching for it. Odds are, the next note will be back in your original four-fret area.

I had a student tell me he used this techinque while waiting oustide the door at an audition. By the time it was his turn to play, he'd learned the tune.

10 GOT PHASE?

If you're playing on stages with PA's, make sure you're in phase with the PA before you play. When you're out of phase, the bass cabinet and the PA's cabinets will cancel each other out, and you won't be able to hear yourself. You'll end up turning up real loud and still probably not be able to hear yourself.

Here's how phase works. Two different speakers (in this case, the ones inside your bass cabinet and the ones in the PA cabinet) should intitally move in the same direction to produce the same sound. A simplified explanation is that a speaker creates sound waves by pushing air out and pulling air back in. When two different speakers are out of phase, the first direction one speaker travels to create sound will be by pulling air in while the initial travel of the other speaker will be to push air out. Listened to in isolation, each speaker will sound fine. But when the sound waves from both speakers arrive at your eardrum simultaneously, the two will cancel each other out because they'll be asking your eardrum to travel in equally opposing directions at once. When this happens on stage, you'll find yourself compensating by turning up your amp so that you can hear yourself while the rest of the house is getting a heavy dose of stage volume from the unsuspecting bassist...you.

To check if you're in phase with the PA, turn the master volume on your amp down and have the sound engineer turn up your bass in the PA. While playing an open low string, gradually turn up the volume of your amp. If you notice the bass and low end getting louder, then you're in phase. But if the sound gets weaker as you turn up, you're out of phase with the PA.

The way to fix phase problems is to simply switch the polarity (the positive and negative) of one of the speakers. Sometimes the mixing board will have a phase switch so you can check and fix it that way. But that's not always an option. Most amplifiers and some speaker cabinets have banana connections that will allow you to switch the polarity of the cabinets. If you have a self-contained "combo" amp, then usually there's a cable hard-wired from the amp to the cabinet that you can unplug. Make a short cable that allows you to plug into it, and then into your cabinet, that switches the polarity.

11 LIVE MONITOR MIX

On stages where monitors are used, the first thing I ask for is hi-hat. Once that's set, I'll ask for some overheads and have them turn up the side with the ride cymbal (the side that's away from me). Usually, the kick and snare are blasting through the PA, so adding that to the monitors just drowns out the more critical time-keeping sounds like hi-hat and ride cymbal.

12 TOOL KIT LIST

fuses	for your amp and any other rack gear
9V batteries	for active bass electronics, tuners, effects pedals (yours or the guitarist's)
mag-lite	for dark stages – checking out wiring problems on the back of amps, or when the singer loses a contact lens
screwdrivers	phillips and flathead, large and small
allen wrenches	to fit saddle screws and also your truss rod
wire cutters	can't change strings without 'em
super glue	to fix a broken guitar nut, knob, pickguard, strap, or even a fingernail
electrical tape	always handy
zip-ties	to clean up sloppy cable routing or fix a busted pants belt
band-aids	you never know

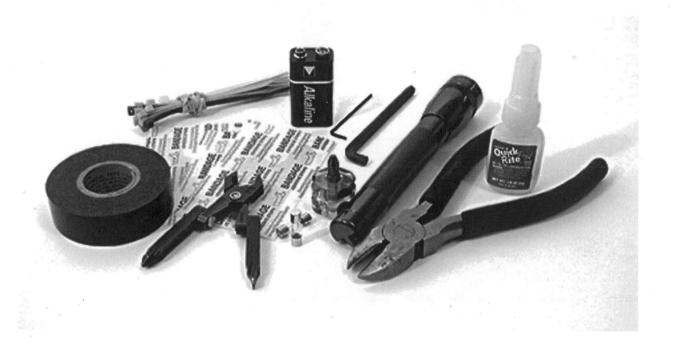

13 MENTAL GAMES

Sometimes it happens...you're on a gig, it might even pay well, but you're bored out of your mind... It's time to get busy. Try playing a tune with only your first finger on your left hand, or only two, three, or four. Try playing a tune without using your first finger on your left hand, just two, three, and four. Play the chorus using only one string. Or, play a tune using only your second and third fingers on your right hand. Just because the music isn't challenging, doesn't mean you can't improve.

14 BEND NEW STRINGS

Bigger strings (A, E, and B if you've got a 5-string) tend to resist being bent over the saddle when they're new. Check to see that they make a straight line from the saddle. If not, push down from the top and re-tune.

Before

Press down at saddle

After

Sometimes the same thing happens at the nut, but usually only on the B string. Press down on either side of the nut, and you'll get it to straighten out.

15 RE-USE FRETLESS STRINGS

If you're changing strings on a fretless and a fretted, you can squeeze a little more life out of the fretless set by putting them on the fretted. Since they haven't been "indented" at all the fret contact points, they can sound a little more "alive" than if you tried boiling the fretted set for reuse. Better yet, boil the fretless set, then put them on the fretted.

16 RUBBING ALCOHOL

If you find that your strings are dying too fast, you might want to keep your hands dry by using ordinary rubbing alcohol right before every time you play or practice. It makes a good instrument /string cleaner, and it's cheap too. It's not an issue of personal hygiene, it's just that some people have a body chemistry that results in more oil emitting from their hands than others. I'm lucky in that respect. I could be out in humid 90° weather, and my hands would stay perfectly dry… Go figure.

17 STRING-TO-STRING BALANCE

One of the most important things about bass setup is the volume balance from string to string. Improper string-to-string balance can really make it difficult for your right hand to play every note at the volume you want efficiently. This involves adjusting individual strings and also adjustment of the pickup heights. The first thing to look for is whether your strings are lined up with the curve of the neck.

Here are a few strings that are out of balance and need adjustment.

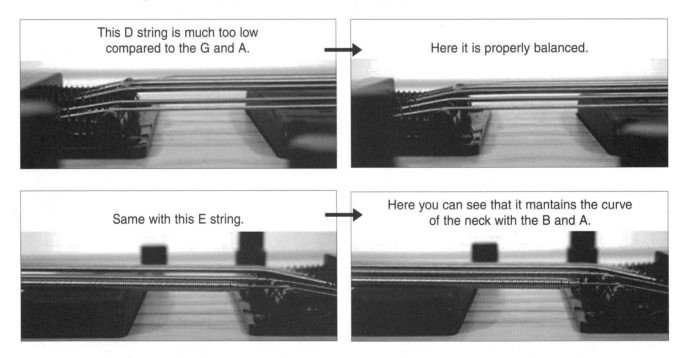

This D string is much too low compared to the G and A. → Here it is properly balanced.

Same with this E string. → Here you can see that it mantains the curve of the neck with the B and A.

Adjust your strings to match the curve in the neck, but make sure they play evenly without creating more buzzes or getting all the strings too high.

Once the strings are adjusted properly, you need to make sure the pickups give you balanced output. Isolate one pickup at a time, and play a scale from your lowest string to your highest string. If you notice an increase or decrease in volume, you need to adjust the height of that pickup. Obviously, the closer the pickup is to the strings, the louder the strings will be.

If you find that a pickup is not moving toward the strings when you loosen the screws, you'll need to place foam underneath it to help hold it up. Carefully remove the screws and pull out the pickup. (You'll need to loosen the strings.) Cut a small piece of foam and place it on the side of the pickup that needs raising.

Some older pickups have extra-strong magnets in them that prevent adjusting them too close to the string. If you notice a warbled pitch coming from a string that gets worse the higher you play, then your pickup is too close to the strings.

18 ADJUST YOUR INTONATION

Adjusting the intonation on a fretted or fretless is a very simple operation. All you need is a tuner and a screwdriver. Basic intonation is done by adjusting the length of the string so that a note played at the 12th fret is in tune (that is, it matches the natural harmonic at that fret).

Turning the long screw at the back of the bridge will move the saddle forwards or backwards for intonation adjustments. Other bridge systems may have different mechanisms for moving the saddle forwards or backwards, but this method is the most common. Here's how it's done. Tune up the string and then play it at the 12th fret:

- If the note at the 12th fret is *sharp*, the string is too *short*.
- Make the string *longer* by moving the saddle away from the neck.
- Tune up the string and try again.

- If the note at the 12th fret is flat, the string is too long.

- Make the string *shorter* by moving the saddle towards the neck.

- Tune up the string and try again.

On a fretless, you should adjust the intonation according to how *you* want to play in relationship to the lines.

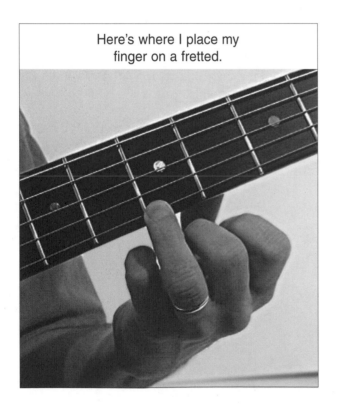

Here's where I place my finger on a fretted.

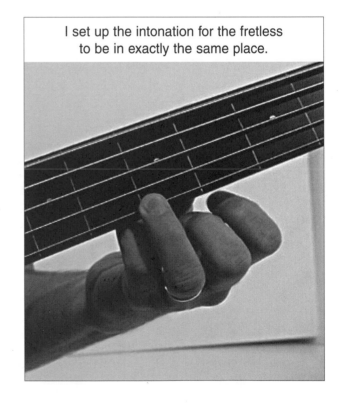

I set up the intonation for the fretless to be in exactly the same place.

It's important to realize that to play in tune on a fretless, you have to adjust your finger placement depending on which part of the neck you're playing. It's common for people to set fretless intonation so that a note is in tune when the line is directly in the middle of the finger. If this is done for the 12th fret, it forces you to play very sharp (past the line) in the lower registers.

If you set it like this
for the 12th fret:

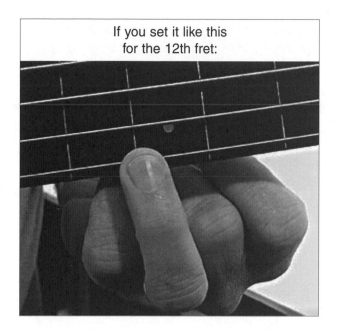

You might have to play like this in
the first few frets:

Setting the intonation with the finger slightly behind the 12th fret gets these results:

12th fret
adjusted for slightly
behind the line

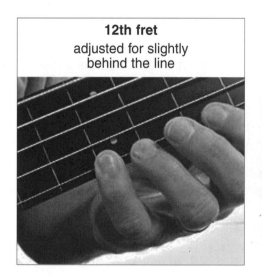

2nd fret
lines up in the
center of the finger

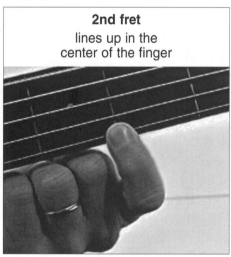

21st fret
much more
behind the line

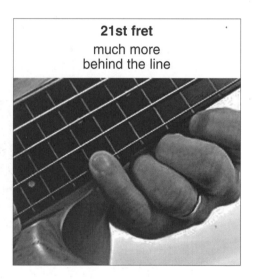

19 LOCATION, LOCATION

Unfortunately, a lot of bassists tend to find a place they're comfortable with for the right hand and stay there. There's a whole range of different tones available by playing from down near the bridge to up over the neck. Closer to the bridge will get you a punchy midrange tone that will help your notes cut. The other extreme is up on the heel of the neck.

You have to adjust your right-hand intensity for this new range of positions. There's more resistance to your right hand closer to the bridge, so be careful about playing there all the time. It can lead to too much tension—and tendonitis—in your right hand. The strings are much looser feeling up over the neck, so you have to tone down your intensity or you'll be slamming the strings down onto the neck for every note—a legitimate effect, but make sure you're in control.

20 GO LOW

Lower = Bigger

On a 4-string bass, especially when you're playing in the keys between E and G, don't get stuck in the upper register all the time. Of course, some grooves and patterns require that you have that string available below the root, but some clever transposition will allow you to play the same ideas down low so the band's spectrum from low to high will sound broader.

If you're new to a 5- or 6-string bass, don't avoid those extra low notes. Spend time getting comfortable playing in the keys of E♭ down to B with those low roots.

There are times, of course, when you'll want to save those extra low notes for just the right part of the tune, but otherwise make it a habit to hang out down there and get comfortable. Bigger is better. For 5- and 6-string players: Be aware of the difference in tones when you play, for instance, in the key of C on the A string and C on the E string. Higher up the neck but on a bigger string will get you a darker, fuller tone that may be just what's needed for certain tunes.

21 FRETLESS READING

Some consider it cheating, but I say use all the help you can get. If you find yourself reading on fretless and you don't feel like you've developed that perfect-intonation muscle memory we all strive for (I know I'm not there yet), then position the music stand so that the neck sits directly between your eyes and the music. That way, a quick glance at the neck won't interfere with keeping your place on the chart.

22 NUT HEIGHT

Try this test on your bass. You'll need a third hand to help you out.

Play some ideas on the lowest part of your neck, something involving the 1st fret—for instance, an F# major scale. Then have someone hold down all the strings on the 1st fret (like a capo) and play the same ideas up a fret. Feel different?

That's how your bass could feel if the nut was cut accordingly.

Look at the distance the string moves when you fret the first fret on each string. Then look at how much each string moves when you hold down the first fret and fret the second fret. That's how low the nut could/should be.

There are a couple of solutions. You can buy a set of fret files and file down the slots individually. Or, if all the strings seem to be the same distance above the neck, you can sand the bottom of the nut to remove enough material to make all the strings lower. Either way is risky and requires some basic skill and experience since you could damage the nut and possibly render it useless. If you have any doubts, take it to a pro. Hopefully, the tech will be the kind of person who will let you watch the process so that you can try it yourself next time. Some bass designs alleviate this problem by including a Zero Fret: a fret located where the nut normally is, with the nut slightly behind.

23 STRING TRIMMING

For newer, smaller Gotoh™ type tuners, you only need to leave about 2 to 3 inches of string to wrap around the tuning peg. When installing new strings, here's how much string to cut:

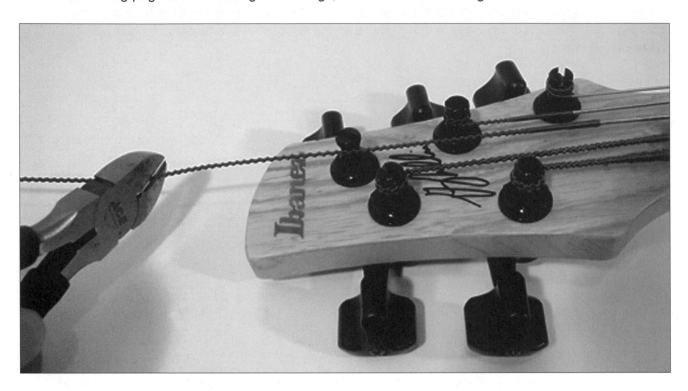

For older Fender™ style tuners, you can basically leave the string intact since the extra wraps around the post help provide the grip to keep the string secure. To save time, before you start winding, insert the end of the string into the peg and wrap the extra string around the post until there's just enough room to bend the string down over one of the slotted edges.

24 PARAMETRIC PARAMETERS

Having a fundamental understanding of how a parametric EQ works is valuable in a number of situations. Bass amps, guitar amps, PA mixing boards, or the mixing desk of a recording studio are the most common situations where you'll find parametric EQ devices. Most importantly, knowing the ins and outs of Parametric EQ allow you to get the best sound out of your own gear, plus it'll help when you need to interact with PA and studio engineers who are responsible for translating your sound to the audience or on to tape. There are 3 main elements of a fully parametric EQ: frequency, level, and bandwidth. A fully parametric EQ will give you control over all three of these parameters, thus the name.

Frequency is the central pitch of the area that you want to change. This unit has two bands of parametric EQ. The top one operates in the 180 to 1.2k range, while the lower band is adjustable from 1.3k to 7.5k. An open A string vibrates at 60Hz… That's 60 times a second, which is considered to be in the range of "low" freqencies. Lows, mids, and highs are relative to each instrument, but mids on a bass are considered to be in the 500Hz to 1,200Hz range (also expressed as 1.2kHz). Highs on a bass are everything above that. Once you get above around 500Hz, you're not actually dealing with the fundamental pitches of the instrument but the overtones, harmonics, and eventually string noise (once you get above 2kHz).

Level, like it sounds, is simply raising or lowering the frequencies or area of frequencies you're trying to change. The boost or cut is measured in dB (decibels). A 3dB boost is described as twice as loud.

Bandwidth is area on either side of the central pitch that you want to affect. For instance, a wide bandwith boost at 60Hz will sound like you're turning up all the low end. Or, a very narrow bandwidth cut at 1.2kHz will mellow out some "honk" in the upper mids without destroying the basic sound of the instrument.

Knowing the basics of how all three controls work will definitely come in handy every time you're in the studio and want to intelligently talk with an engineer about what's going on with your sound or any other instrument. It's also valuable if you find yourself playing through different amplifiers. Not every amp has fully parametric controls, but the ability to quickly dial up the sound you want makes rehearsals, soundchecks, and gigs a lot more painless.

25 BASS REVERB EQ

A full-range reverb sounds great on a bass by itself, but in order for it to sound clear in a track or on stage you need to EQ the reverb itself. In the studio, you can patch the reverb through an EQ or return it to its own tracks for EQ. I've gotten the best results by rolling off everything below 500hz. That way you get the shimmer and spaciousness without the muddy lows rumbling around and clouding things up. Live, you probably won't have the luxury of running your reverb through a separate EQ, so just make sure the unit has EQ as one of the editable parameters. If that's not available, some will let you set the decay time of the low frequencies separately from the rest. That way you can shorten the decay of the lows and clear up the effect.

26 BASS TRACKING

When recording a bass track, try to send as pure a signal as possible to the tape machine. Go through as few electronic devices as possible, including the mixing board. The less signal processing you record with, the more flexibility you'll have to try different EQ's and effects later on.

Of course, the signal has to come back from the machine into the board so that you and others can monitor it, but at that point you're free to EQ and affect the sound without being stuck with the results on tape. If listening to your effects is critical to your performance, send the dry signal (preferably right from the direct box) to tape and the effects that you're monitoring to a second bass track. Again, you won't be stuck with the processed signal, and you'll be free to try other effects, a different wet/dry mix, or no effects at all.

Since highs are a lot more predominant in headphones than what I'm used to hearing from a bass amp, I'll have the engineer reduce the frequencies from 2kHz and up while I'm tracking, and then we'll listen to playback with no EQ.

27 CABLE DISCIPLINE

A well-trained cord is always well behaved and doesn't get involved in intimate relationships with other cords.

Do your cords look like this?	Make them look like this:
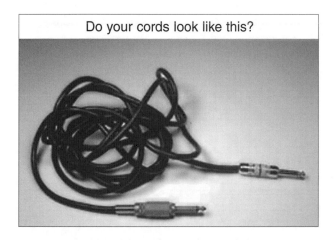	

Spare the twist, spoil the cord:

Give it a little clockwise twist as you wrap it with your right hand, and it'll learn to avoid the tangles and kinks that come from a bad upbringing.

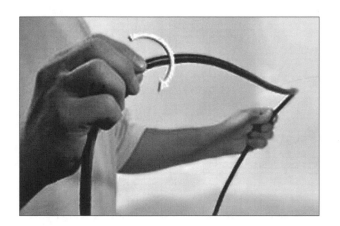 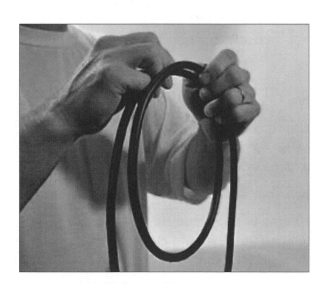

28 TWEETER ADJUSTMENT

A lot of modern speaker cabinet designs come with a tweeter whose volume is adjustable from the back of the cabinet. These passive designs use the variable resistance within a coil to change the volume of the tweeter. Unfortunately, if you turn down the volume of the tweeter in this passive design, the amplifier's signal is going through fewer turns of the coil and the coil is more likely to heat up and cause problems. Instead of reducing the volume of the tweeter at the cabinet, run it flat (the middle setting) and use the EQ controls of the amp to reduce the treble.

29 THE SOUND OF WOOD

One of the biggest factors in determining the overall sound and response of a bass is the wood, especially the body wood. Learn how different woods behave, and make that a part of your decision in choosing your next instrument.

- Heavy (dense) woods do a good job of compressing the overall sound and evening things up.

- Lighter (less dense) woods like alder and ash generally have a wider response from softs to louds, and their resonant frequency is closer to the bass tones you're trying to produce.

  Since different playing styles require different characteristics from a bass, choose your next instrument accordingly.

30 COMPRESS FOR FINESSE

Don't use the compressor when playing with your fingers. Switch it in when you slap, but out when you go back to fingerstyle playing. That way, you'll save your right-hand fingerstyle technique from having to compete with the volume of your own funky spankin'.

31 DYNAMICS VS. EVEN

Everyone always talks about how important it is to get your eighth and sixteenths notes even, but what's missing in a lot of this talk is dynamics. The differences in individual volumes in a line are what gives a groove or a line its life and really affects the feel. Here's a simple exercise to get you working on dynamics in your right-hand technique.

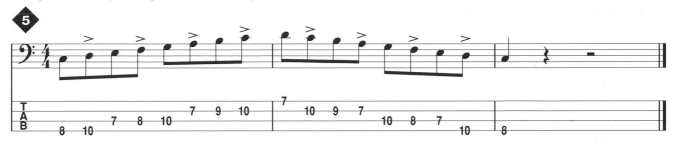

Here's the same exercise played with a swing feel.

This deceptively simple exercise is meant to be played as slow as necessary to execute the details. First of all, you should play these notes *legato*. That means absolutely no gaps in between the notes. In the first exercise, the first eighth note of every pair is soft, and the second eighth note is always louder (not loud). In the second exercise, the first eighth note of every pair is soft and long, and the second eighth note is always short and louder. Don't try to kill the loud note, just play the first note really soft so that you can start exploring the other end of the volume spectrum. After working on dynamics for a while, you'll discover that getting everything even will be easy.

32 MIRROR, MIRROR...

Watch yourself practicing in a mirror. Once you get over how good you look, unnecessary finger movement (especially in the left hand), technique flaws, and bad technique in general really jump out at you when you're watching from a different perspective.

33 MAKE YOUR OWN STRAP

A good, wide custom-fit strap helps eliminate fatigue and is actually easy to make.

1) First you need the raw material. Ask for Latigo, and specify 2 ounce or bigger. That's about 1/8" thick. Latigo has a finished shiny side and an unfinished suede-like side that won't slide off your shoulder. If there's not a hobby or craft store in your area, try www.auburnleather.com (800-635-0617). A 5" width will distribute the weight of the bass on your shoulder better. To find out what length to order, measure your current strap from hole to hole and add at least 8 inches. The leftover leather is used for reinforcement.

 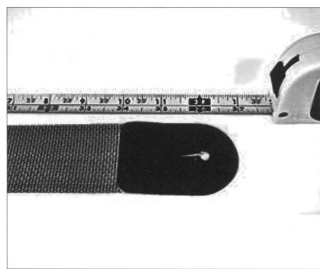

2) Cut the length 2" longer than your hole-to-hole measurement. After that, make two cuts so that the general shape of the strap will look like this:

The first cut is determined by the distance from the end pin to the center of your shoulder. Make a cut that leaves 2 1/2" of width on the end to the full width of the strap at the distance you measured. Then cut from there to the other end, also leaving 2 1/2" of width.

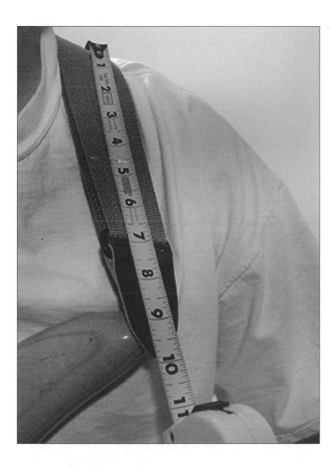

3) Cut the holes an inch from the end of the strap. If you don't have a hole punch, a pair of wire cutters will work just as well. Fashion a hole about 1/4" in diameter with a slit similar to this shape:

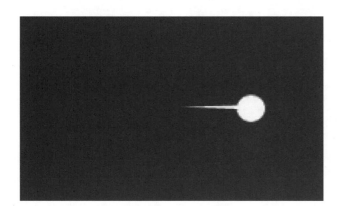

4) Use the leftover leather and glue a 3" piece on each end with rubber cement to reinforce the strap holes. Trim away the excess, and you're done.

34 | 2-5=5

When you're improvising over ii-V progressions, except for the movement of one note, you can just imagine playing over the V chord and still get good results. In a progression with a lot of ii-Vs, this will reduce the amount of chords you have to think about, allowing you to play longer ideas that aren't interrupted every time there's a chord change. The one note to be careful with if you're just thinking of the V chord is its major 3rd. For instance, the V of C is G7. Its 3rd is B, which is the 6th or 13th of Dm7 (the ii of C). The sound of that B over a Dm7 will create more tension than any of the other diatonic chord tones of Dm7—but only if the chord lasts a long time (like four beats at a slow tempo). If the ii-Vs are going by faster, as in two beats each per bar, then you're less likely to notice the tension, and the B will sound more like it "belongs" to your ideas.

For each ii-V in this progression, I center my ideas around the 5th:

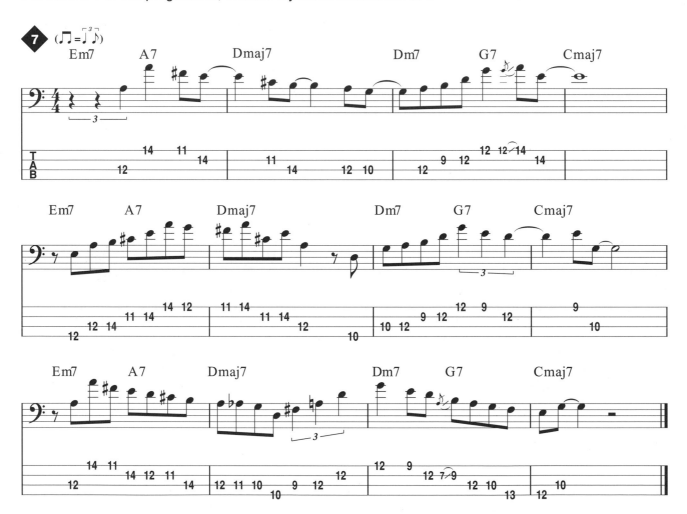

Here's the same progression for you to work on.

35 7SUS CHORDS

When playing over a 7sus chord, you have to consider your role before you decide what to do. Your choice as a soloist will be different than your choice as a bassist/accompanyist. Think of the 7sus sound as a minor or major 7th chord with a different note in the bass. For instance, a Dm7 (all four voices: 1-3-5-7) with a G in the bass will produce a G7sus chord.

The 1-3-5-7 of Dm7 become the 5th, 7th, 9th, and 11th of G7sus. The 7th of D (the C) provides the "sus" part of the sound. The relative major of D minor is F major, so an Fmaj7 with that same G in the bass will also give you a G7sus sound.

Technically it could be called a G13sus with the 1-3-5-7 of Fmaj7 providing the 7th, 9th, 11th, and 13th of the G7sus chord.

Another way to describe these two voicings is as a minor 7th with the 4th in the bass or a major 7th with the 2nd in the bass. Here's where your role comes in. Obviously, your role as a bassist is to supply the roots. Play the root at the beginning of the bar, and then use the chord tones of the "other" 7th chord in the rest of the bar. For a G7sus, play the G at the beginning and then think of Dmi7 or Fmaj7 for the rest of the bar.

Here's an example of a bass line over a D7sus–F7sus progression.

* indicates 5th string on a 5-string bass

As a soloist you should be trying to sound "above" the harmony, so only think of the m7 or the maj7 chord as it relates to the root of the 7sus chord. For instance, over G7sus, just think of the Dm7 and/or Fmaj7.

Here's an example of a solo over the previous progression.

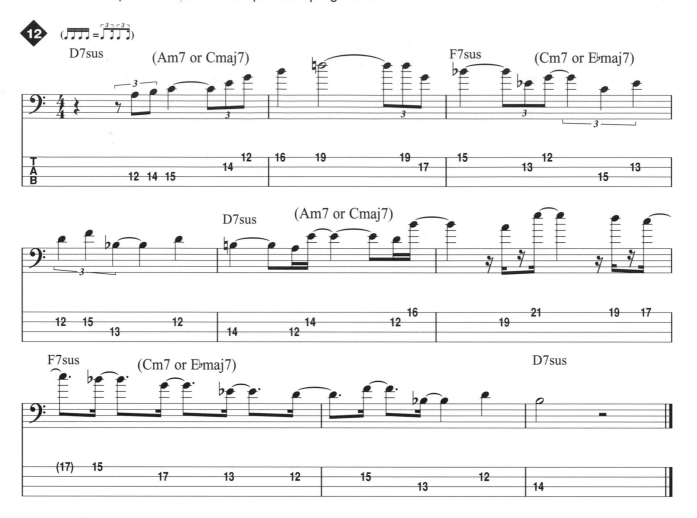

Here's the progression for you to practice with.

36 GAIN STRUCTURE

Getting the gain structure right in a bass system means optimizing the output of all the various amplifiers that are involved, in order to get them operating at their most efficient settings, so that you can get the best sounding signal to the speaker or tape machine… In other words: you have to get a bunch of knobs right.

In a simple setup, you'll have the volume knob on your bass, an input knob on the amp, and a master volume knob on the amp. Each knob controls amplifier circuitry that feeds the next one. The higher you turn up the knob or gain on an amplifier circuit, the less efficient that amp becomes and the worse it will sound. Amplifier circuitry requires headroom in order to reproduce the wide range of dynamics that are coming out of your bass. (You do use dynamics when you play, right?) The most critical of these is the input control on your amplifier. That's why most amps with this control also give you an indicator (usually an LED light) that changes color to help you adjust the input level to its most optimum setting. Other, simpler setups offer two different jacks that you can plug into: active or passive.

You mainly want to avoid any extremes for any of the knobs—except perhaps the bass output knob. Too much output from your bass might cause you to have to turn down the input stage and force you to compensate by really cranking the master volume; turning the input stage way down and then amplifying it back up with the master will increase the amount of noise you hear. Too little output from the bass will cause you to have to really turn up the input stage to a level where that input amplifer section runs out of headroom and the efficiency you need from it. Once you have the proper relationship set between the output of the bass and the input stage of the amp, use the master volume as much as possible to adjust your overall volume. If you rely too much on the volume knob of the bass, you'll upset the balance and efficiency that's achieved by dialing in the output/input relationship.

How loud should you turn up your bass? The standard output level that manufacturers used for years was the old standby Fender Jazz® bass. With the preamps on basses starting to incorporate 18-volt (dual 9-volt battery) systems, it's becoming increasingly possible to really overdrive the input stage of your amplifier. If you don't happen to have an old '63 Jazz laying around, take your bass to a music store and compare the output volumes. New amplifier input circuitry is more and more designed to handle the increased output of the newer active bass circuitry, but you should still try to optimize the settings in order to get the most out of your system.

TIPS 37 – 39 : SETTING UP YOUR OWN ACTION

No, I don't mean you have to know "Vegas Vinnie's" cell number.

"Action" in this case means the playability of your bass. Part of it is setting up the right amount of relief in the neck, which is controlled by the truss rod. The other part involves string height, which is adjusted with the individual saddles on the bridge. Both of these adjustments tend to intimidate a lot of bassists, but they're relatively easy to master once you understand the basics. Understanding the basic relationships between string height and neck relief is the first step, so it's tip #37. Tips #38 and 39 show you how to adjust these two elements.

37 STRING HEIGHT/NECK RELIEF

String height and neck relief are related. You can't adjust one without affecting the other, so here's where understanding the basics comes into play. Take a look at how a string vibrates.

A string vibrates in a slight but long curve througout the length of the string. That's why there needs to be some *relief* or *bow* in the neck to compensate for this curve and allow the string to vibrate freely but stay close to the neck.

Here's how you can find out how much bow is in your neck:

• Hold down the A string at the first fret with your first finger.

• Then, just past the end of the neck, hold down the A string against the neck with your elbow.

When you press the string against the neck at the first fret and at the end of the neck, you've created a perfectly straight line. How much that line (string) can move tells you how much relief is in the neck. While the string is held down at both ends of the neck, use your first finger on your right hand to tap on the string. The amount it moves is how much relief is in the neck.

How much should it move?

On my bass, it moves about the thickness of a credit card. You want it to at least move a little. If it doesn't move at all, then you need to loosen the truss rod.

How much is too much?

The best way to tell if the right amount of relief is in your neck is to lower the strings.

• If after lowering the strings, the notes buzz only above the 12th fret, then there's too much bow in the neck. You'll need to tighten the truss rod.

• If after you lower the strings, the notes only buzz in the first five frets, then your neck is too straight. You'll need to loosen the truss rod.

• If after you lower the strings, the notes buzz all up and down the neck, the neck's fine. Your strings are just too low.

A truss rod is actually two metal bars crammed into an exact fit underneath the fingerboard. The normal configuration is that the end of one of the pieces is threaded with an an adjusting screw or nut and passes through a sleeve welded to the other one. Once the screw or nut is tightened, it bends the other bar and, because of the tight fit, the whole neck. In addition to providing the ability to adjust the amount of relief in the neck, a truss rod gives the wooden neck support so it can withstand the tension caused by the metal strings. You can adjust the truss rod by turning the nut that sits underneath the fingerboard at the headstock or by turning the screw that's accessed at the heel of the neck.

Loosening the truss rod

If the truss rod adjustment is located at the headstock, you may need to loosen and move a string out of the way.

Important! Turn the trust rod adjustment counter-clockwise only 1/4 turn. You should be able to see a difference after a quarter turn. If not, try a little more, but I'd recommend no more than a half a turn per day. Wooden necks require time to "settle in" to truss rod adjustments.

Tightening the truss rod

Tightening is a little more complicated. Before you turn the wrench, you need to "help" straighten the neck a little. This is easiest if you're sitting down.

* Stand the bass on the floor.

* Put your foot in front of it.

* Put your knee behind it.

* Carefully push on the front of the headstock.

Then, while you're putting pressure on the headstock, make your adjustment clockwise to tighten the truss rod.

Important! Again, only turn it clockwise 1/4 of a turn. You should be able to see a difference after a quarter turn. If not, try a little more, but I'd still recommend no more than a half a turn a day.

39 ADJUSTING STRING HEIGHT

One of the side effects of adjusting the truss rod is that the height of the strings is also changed.

• Tightening the truss rod lowers the string height.

• Loosening the truss rod raises the string height.

To compensate for these changes, or to affect the action along the entire length of the bass neck (once the relief is set), you'll need to adjust the height of the strings.

You adjust the string height by raising or lowering the saddles where each string rests at the bridge.

I try to lower the strings as much as possible but still keep them from buzzing. Play every note on a string from the first fret to the highest when you're checking for buzzes. On a fretless, if the strings are adjusted too high, fretless notes lose their characteristic "buzz." When they're adjusted too low, the extra "buzz" chokes the note and doesn't let it "breathe" Some buzzing on a fretted is acceptable because, although it might be audible acoustically while you're setting up your action, it's not so noticeable when the sound comes out of your amp.

Almost all fingerboards are constructed with a slight curve or "radius." When you're adjusting the strings, make sure they follow the radius of the neck (see tip #17). Also, the larger strings need to be set up just slightly higher than the rest. If you set up your string height correctly, you should be able to observe this radius from the side. Hold the body horizontally, and look closely at the strings. You should be able to see each string come into view as you slowly turn the bass towards you. This means that the strings are following the radius of the neck.

(40) FRETLESS PRACTICE

Record a "drone"—an open string played constantly enough so that you don't hear it decay—and practice fretless along with it. For instance, record your open G as a drone and play along with the recording. Make sure your playback device is in tune. If not, use the G to re-tune your bass. You can start by playing G major scales very slowly. Be careful that each note you play is in tune. Make sure you work on different registers as well. You can also use C major, E minor, G minor, C minor, etc.

Here's a G drone for you to practice with.

41 FRETLESS PIVOT

On fretless, the ability to pivot on the tips of your fingers with the left hand will improve your intonation and vibrato. Once you've set up your intonation on a fretless (tip #18) you'll have a good idea for where to put your finger to play a note in tune. If you don't happen to hit that spot with deadly accuracy all the time (believe me, it'll happen), then you'll need a way to coax the note to the right pitch without sliding. This is where the pivot comes in. Think of it as the needle on a tuner that's searching for the right pitch.

The pivot is accomplished by controlling the movement of each finger from the knuckle joint at your hand. The tip of your finger will "roll" parallel to the string and cause the note to go sharp or flat. This may not come naturally at first, so make sure that you're not moving your whole hand to get this to work. Eventually you should be able to control the pivot for each finger independently.

Even if you do get your finger in exactly the right spot, a fretless note needs to have a little movement in order to retain its musical character. Practice moving away and returning with your pivot in a very slow and controlled manner. Try both sides of the pitch, sharper and flatter, in order to gain the most control with your fingers.

Start out with just single notes. Play the D, G, C, and F, and pivot regardless of whether you nail the pitch or not. The first four bars are an example of what it sounds like. Notice that I intentionally pivot the note even though it might start out in tune. The rest of the example is for you to practice with.

Later on, try playing octaves and 5ths to get a handle on the pivot with the little finger.

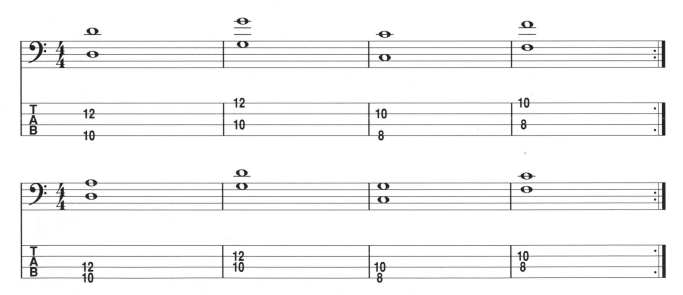

This ability to adjust the pitch is central to having a musical and expressive vibrato. Too often, fretless players neglect to learn this control of their vibrato, and echoes of Ethel Merman are summoned from the grave… God rest her soul. You can, of course, choose whatever vibrato style you prefer, but a fast, out-of-control vibrato loses its musical effect and ends up sounding like a "nervous" habit.

42 A FRETLESS DON'T

I have to remind myself of this one ocasionally. On a fretted bass, it's a common technique in lower registers to pull on the string of a note in the left hand to get a subtle vibrato or pitch movement out of a note. This is a definite no-no on a fretless. You'll be grinding a metal string sideways across an epoxy-coated or possibly bare wooden fingerboard. Eventually the metal will grind away some epoxy or wood, and the useful lifespan of your fingerboard will be compromised. You can get the same kind of pitch movement by moving your finger parallel to the string, and it causes little if no wear on the fingerboard.

43 THE LOCTITE SOLUTION

Ever notice your that your string height becomes drastically different after you change strings? Even if you used the same brand and gauge? What's happened is that when you remove a string, the saddle adjustment screws become loose and easy to turn. The vibration or buzz that you hear when you pull a string (most likely a roundwound) through the hole at the back of the bridge can cause these loose adjustment screws to spin, and your carefullly adjusted string height becomes all out of whack.

Once you've got your string height set where you want it, use some blue (272) medium strength LocTite on the screws, and they'll stay put. The medium strength will allow you to still make adjustments from time to time but can prevent the out of control spinning whenever you change strings.

Here's how to apply the LocTite once your string height is set:

- You need to expose the part of the screw that's being used in order to get the LocTite applied correctly.

- Extend the screw through the bottom of the saddle exactly three turns.

- Apply a small amount of LocTite to the threads nearest the saddle.

- Retract the screw back up into the saddle exactly three turns.

    This will maintain whatever adjustments you've made but insure the LocTite is in contact with the threads and the inside of the saddle.

If you really don't want to use the LocTite, you can physically hold the saddle against the bridge whenever you pull a string through, and this will help keep the saddle screws in place. Just make sure you only change one string at a time.

44 NO TV!

OK, you're not grounded. But here's the rule:

Do not watch TV while you run your scales and arpeggios and call it practicing. You'll be basically training your brain to ignore what your hands are doing the whole time. Hey, your brain is smart; it can usually keep track of letting your hands switch to automatic pilot while the other part of your brain is processing "Bay Watch" (that's while the bass is in your hands, of course). But you won't be getting any better at the bass. If you feel like your brain isn't challenged when you practice, then blow off those scales and arpeggios and start creating your own exercises. By giving practicing your undivided attention and applying concentrated, problem-solving, creative mental energy, you'll get a lot more accomplished and probably in a shorter amount of time.

45 STEEL WOOL TRICK

Use #00 "Double-Ought" steel wool on the back of your bass neck. Make sure you neck is clean first (#16) and then just rub it parallel to the neck. You'll find the neck much "slicker" and easier to play. Be careful not to rub against the body, since it can turn a glossy finish into a less shiny "satin" finish. #0000 "Four-Ought" steel wool will give you the same results, but its finer finish seems to wear away and lose its effect sooner.

46 TWO-FINGER TEST

Wondering if that fret buzz is because of a bad fret? Here's a little test that can tell you what's going on.

If you've set up your fingerboad truss rod adjustment according to tip #38, then your neck will have a slight bow to it. That means that out of any three adjacent frets, the middle one should be just slightly lower than the other two—that's if you draw a straight line across the top of the outer two frets. In this case, we can use an existing string to create that straight line. The middle fret should be just low enough for the string to ring, or you should be able to hear the string "click" against the middle fret if you tap on it.

Think of it as creating a little 3-fret neck. Select the three frets you want to use, place a finger outside of the 1st and 3rd fret, and press down. Play the "note" that you've created or try tapping on that middle fret. You should be able to hear a very high pitch when you play it. Or if you tap on it, you should be able to hear a barely audible click caused by the string hitting the fret.

Try moving this two finger, 3-fret configuration up and down the neck. If you find a dead "note" or a fret that won't "click", it means you've found a fret that's too high or that the fret in front of it is too low. The good news is that you've located the problem. The bad news is that it's probably going to require some fretwork to fix it. Unfortunately, fretwork is beyond the scope of this book and should be left to professionals. You can compensate by raising your string height, but this shouldn't be considered a long-term solution.

It's possible to squeeze the heck out of the neck with left hand, and the only results are that you're inviting tendonitis and making the bass very difficult to play. By learning about accuracy in tip #47 and teaching your hand relaxation with tip #48, you can make left-hand fatigue a thing of the past and greatly increase your mobility on the neck.

④⑦ LEFT-HAND ACCURACY

Try this experiment on a fretted bass. Put your first finger directly over the dot that's in between the B and C on the A string. Your finger should be exactly in the middle between the two frets.

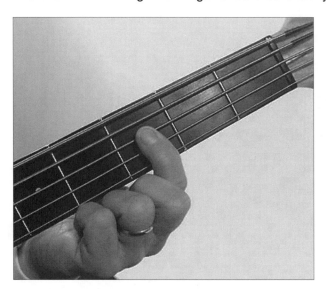

When you press down, the resulting note will be a C. Play constant, repeated C's in the right hand. Try letting up on the pressure and notice how quickly the note wants to start buzzing. Go back and forth from the clean C to the buzz to get a sense of the pressure involved. Now move your finger up to the C so that your finger is on or just slightly past the 3rd fret.

Play the constant C's and try letting up on the pressure again. Notice anything different?

You should be able to tell that as you lift up it doesn't want to buzz nearly as soon as when your finger is directly in the middle between the frets. Again, go back and forth from the clean C to the buzzing.

As you lift up, try to stop just before the C starts to buzz. That amount of pressure, right before it will start to buzz, is all the pressure that's needed to play a note on the bass. Is it less pressure than you normally use? I thought so. Probably a lot less pressure.

By being accurate with the left hand and always having your finger in contact with the fret, you can use a lot less effort to play the bass. Accuracy can be acquired just by being conscious of having your finger in the right place every time you play a note. However, you still need tip #48 to teach your hand how to reduce the amount of pressure involved. Check it out.

48 MINIMUM PRESSURE

Now that you know how to locate your fingers in the left hand to allow you to use less pressure, you need to teach your left hand exactly where that pressure point is for each finger. We'll start with the 2nd finger on a G (E string, 3rd fret). Make sure that you locate that 2nd finger just touching or slightly past the fret you're using. Play constant repeated notes with the right hand just like in #47. Start out with your finger just touching the string (no note should sound) and then gradually press down all the while playing constantly with the right hand. Once the G stops buzzing and sounds cleanly, gradually lift up with the 2nd finger until it begins to buzz again. Keep alternating buzzing and clean until you get a sense of exactly how much pressure it takes to keep the note clean. Always be just on the verge of buzzing. Once you think you have a handle on the pressure, play each note of the G major scale for at least 30 seconds, just barely alternating between buzz and clean. Go up and down the scale at least twice this way. It would be a good idea to start out every practice session with this exercise.

Here's an example of what the G should sound like:

Every once in a while, you can use this next exercise to test how well your fingers are learning the pressure points. Play the same G major scale again. This time, just attack the note once with the right hand, and with the left hand start out the note "clean" without buzzing. Then while it's sustaining, barely lift up the pressure with the left hand until it just starts to buzz, and then return it to its "clean" state. If your fingers have learned the pressure point, you should quickly be able to make it buzz but be able to bring it back to clean without losing the note. If you release too much pressure while trying to get it to buzz, the note will die out. Once you're able to play a scale anywhere on the neck with this "clean-buzz-clean" kind of control, your left hand will be much more efficient. You'll be able to play relaxed for hours at a time and move freely up and down the neck with very little resistance.

Here's an example of what the scale "pressure test" should sound like:

49 PICKUP BALANCE

If your bass has two pickups, then turning both of them all the way up or moving the balance control to the click in the middle doesn't mean that they're balanced.

Here's how much a string moves over a front pickup.

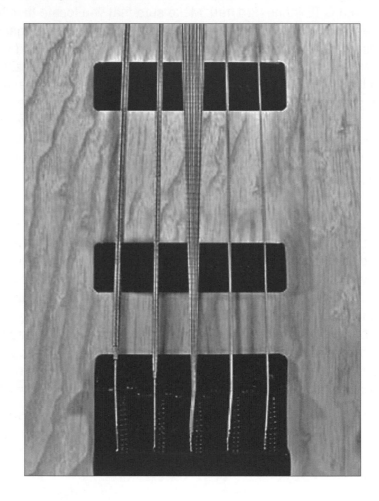

Here's how much the same string moves over a back pickup.

You can see that the string vibrates in a broader path so that the front pickup will always be louder even if they're turned up equally. You've also probably noticed the difference in tones between a front and rear pickup. The front pickup is darker and has more fundamental in the sound, while the rear has more midrange and overtones. In addition to being louder, even at the same setting, the front pickup has a tendency to mask the overtones that come out of the back pickup. If you want a balance of the two, start with the back pickup louder or all the way up, and gradually bring in the front pickup until you hear a balance. Use your ears—don't trust the middle setting or having both knobs all the way up for a proper balance.

50 SHIM THE NECK

Ever tried to lower your strings but you ran out of saddle adjustment room and couldn't get the strings any lower? This is actually a very common problem with a lot of basses, and it has fairly "low-tech" solution. All you need is a screwdriver, scissors, and a business card. By putting a "shim" (spacer) under the heel of the neck, you can slightly change the angle of the neck, creating more room for lowering the strings.

Start by loosening all the strings so that you can get them off the headstock. It's OK to leave the strings in the bridge. Then remove the neck... Usually it's the four screws on the back of the bass. Make sure to keep track of which screw went in each hole. Some screws are shorter than others (you don't want a screw sticking through the front of the neck).

As you take the neck off, be careful to watch and see if a previous shim spacer might fall out. If not, check to see if there's one already in the neck pocket.

It's OK to add to an existing shim. Fold a business card in half lengthwise and trim it to fit into the bottom of the neck pocket.

Use a piece of tape to hold it in place if you want.

Reattach the neck and string it back up. Realize that with the tilt that the shim creates, you've effectively lowered all the strings. You might have to raise the strings at the saddle to get the right height adjustment.

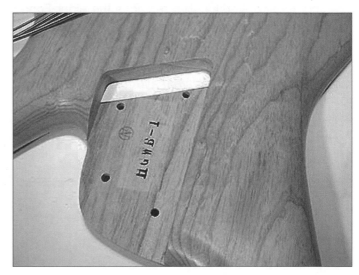

51 WARM UP UNDER CONTROL

If you do get the opportunity to warm up before a gig, it's better to use a headphone amp. Otherwise, if you only hear yourself acoustically, the tendency is to play harder in order to hear yourself, and you'll end up using more tension to get the notes out in warm-up than you'd normally use during a gig. You're basically tensing up instead of warming up. If a headphone amp is out of the question, then just remember to try to get the feeling of playing into your hands, and don't worry about trying to hear yourself acoustically.

52 BASS BALANCE

When you let go of the bass with your hands, the bass should balance by itself. A lot of basses tend to be neck- or headstock-heavy, so you end up having to use your forearm to hold the body down so that the neck will stay up. This support becomes a handicap for your right hand and arm, preventing it from making the shifts necessary to get to the upper and lower strings. If the bass you play is out of balance, your options are limited. Older Fender® style machine heads are heavier than later model tuners and present the most problems, especially when you've chosen a bass that has a light body. One solution is to weight the body. A small amount of lead weight attached to the inside of the electronics cavity will help maintain a balance. The weights can be found at model train stores or hobby shops and since they attach with tape, you won't be ruining the condition of a vintage instrument.

Since companies are starting to manufacture lighter tuners, replacement is another option. Hipshot is making a lighter version that replaces the older Fender® style tuners. On my signature bass, the tuner wings are fitted with metal-plated ABS plastic Sure-Grip® knobs that further lighten the headstock.

www.hipshotproducts.com

www.garywillis.com/pages/bass/tuner.html

53 NO THUMB

This one serves as a reminder to keep the amount of pressure from your thumb to a minimum.

Play normally with your left hand but keep your thumb from contacting the back of the neck. This makes it impossible to "squeeze" the neck. This squeezing can creep into your technique gradually without you noticing. Use this approach ocasionally to make sure this problem stays under control.

54 SOLO SHAPE

When you're working on soloing, it's normal to pick a set of changes or a tune and go for it… chorus after chorus… over and over. Hopefully after twenty or thirty minutes or an hour, you feel like you've improved your vocabulary for that tune. But it's not likely that you'll get the opportunity to play that twenty-minute solo. You'll either get fired, get the band fired, or it's your gig to begin with and nobody cares, including the three people in the audience.

In most settings, a bass solo will usually be a few to a handful of choruses. Some solos don't involve choruses and are just over one chord, so another way to look at it is that there is a limit to the amount of time you should take to get your ideas across. You should practice with this time frame in mind. If you're soloing over 32-bar choruses, try limiting it to three times and organize what you have to say within that framework. If it's over one chord, limit yourself to two minutes and try to build and end your solo within that amount of time.

Your goal should be to "build" a solo. It should have a beginning, a middle, and an end. Generally this involves starting out deliberately, building to what the listener can perceive as a climax, and then ending (see #7). The obvious thing to avoid is too much activity or intensity too soon. You'll lose the sense that the solo is going anywhere. If you have some chops or you want to include some playing in the upper register, save that for later in the solo where it's usually more effective. The shape or contour of a solo is basically accomplished with contrast. Contrast slow with fast, low with high, short ideas with long ideas, simple rhythms with complex, syncopated rhythms, basic harmony with more upper structure, tension-oriented harmony. Of course, you don't have to use all these elements in every solo, and not every solo has to have a prescribed formula. But, an awareness of the actual duration of the solo while you practice will help you to use these elements effectively.

55 DRUMS STOP... BAD

You've all heard the story about the tourist on the safari.

Anyway, it doesn't always have to be that way. If you can, discuss your preferences with the drummer and the rest of the band for what you prefer behind your solo. It makes for a more interesting solo if don't have to "outline" the solo for everyone, including yourself. If the changes and comping are happening under your solo, you're more likely to play more interesting ideas that don't involve putting up the obvious signposts. Tell the drummer that it's OK to go to a ride cymbal, even at the beginning of your solo. Drummers instinctively become more active and supportive when they're riding as opposed to the "walking on eggshells" mentality when they're only playing the hi-hat behind the bass solo.

If the rest of the band insists on taking a break during your solo..."Waitress!"... you can offer to do the same and return the favor. With that threat in mind, odds are you'll get all the support you want.

56 REGIONAL NECK ISOLATION

If some areas of the neck are more uncomfortable than others, confine your left hand to those areas for practicing. Work on playing the same ideas and tunes you already know but stay within a 6-fret area. A 6-fret area is guaranteed to contain the chromatic scale, which means that every note of every key is available to you. You might have to do some transposing, but this is integral to understanding the bass and that particular part of the neck.

Another way to practice is to confine yourself to a pair of strings. This will force you to find new ways to look at the same old things you always play and open up new shapes to your hand. Eventually you'll improve you're ability to connect your ideas up and down the strings and across the strings as well.

57 PULL-OFFS

Pull-offs are slightly mislabeled. A pull-off implies that you play a note with the left hand by pulling your finger "off" the string. But instead of pulling off and up into the air above the neck, which is a common mistake, you can get better results by pulling across the string and down onto the neck. Try to make your finger land onto the neck, adjacent to the string, instead of up in the air. You'll end up with a stronger "pull" on the string and a louder attack.

incorrect follow-through

correct follow-through

You can start with a basic hammer-on, pull-off exercise. Fret a note with your first finger, then hammer-on (correctly labeled) with your second finger to get the note a fret above to sound. Now, pull off with your second finger to get the next note. Make sure that your pull-off finger lands on the neck and not up in the air.

You can use your right hand to play the first note but no right hand after that.

Eventually you should include the third and fourth fingers in this exercise. Keep your first finger on the D, and do this same exercise by playing an E with the third finger and an F with the fourth finger.

This next exercise involves all four fingers and is a little more difficult.

play 4 times

Fm7-Bbm7-E♭7-A♭maj7-D♭maj7-G7-Cmaj7

If you memorize tunes this way, you end up with the equivalent of a nineteen-digit phone number. And that only works for the first eight bars and only applies to that one key. If you use function to memorize chord changes, you can reduce the amount of information your "hard drive" has to store and you can apply it to any key. Here's how it works:

Function means how the chord functions in the key. In this case, the first five chord changes are in the same key, so we can use their relationship to the key for a label. We have a **6-2-5-1-4** in the key of A♭. You could revert to the ancient vi7–ii7–V7, etc., but then you're back to memorizing more information than is necessary. It's a common assumption that a "two" chord is the minor seventh chord built on the second degree of a major key. Since this is already a part of our musical vocabulary, the minimalist label "2" will mean the same thing as a ii7 but serves as a more effective shorthand for our purposes. The information for the first five chord changes can now be reduced to this:

6 2 5 1 4

The only thing that is left is how to indicate the key change. The last two changes are a **5-1** in the key of C. After the **6-2-5-1-4**, you could indicate that the key center moves up a major third, but mentally you'd have to return from the 4 chord to the 1, from there go up a major 3rd and from there up a 2nd to the 2 chord. A simpler way to do it is just to indicate the distance from the two chords involved. In this case, the distance is a diminished fifth or a tritone: TT. It looks like this: (TT)

The circle around the distance information helps keep it separate from the chord functions.

Here's how to put the key-change shorthand to use. It's common to look at major keys with the 2nd finger on the root. In this case, if you look at the first five chords and decide they're in the key of A♭, and locate your hand on the neck with your 2nd finger on an A♭, then this consistent view will always have you playing the 4 chord with your 2nd finger. This same consistency will always have you playing a 5 chord with the 2nd finger one string down from the root, or with the 4th finger a string and two frets up, no matter what key you're in.

With this consistent way of viewing keys, all you need is the distance to the new chord. Since you've already looked at the changes and done your analyzing, this consistent approach gives you the correct finger on the correct chord every time. The new shorthand result is the equivalent of an eight-digit telephone number and is transferrable to any key.

6 2 5 1 4 (TT) 5 1

MACHINE CHOPS

Transcribing is an important part of your musical development. Your goal in transcribing should be to get the music off your CD player into your hands. Writing it out is optional, but either process requires listening to the CD. In order to get more efficient at the transcribing process, you need to focus on developing your "chops" on your CD player. It's important to be able to stop your machine immediately after the note or notes you're targeting. Anything your ears hear after the target point becomes confusing, and you usually have to listen again. Stop consistently at the target notes, and the notes stay in your head and are easier to find. Also learn to rewind accurately and consistently. Rewind too far, and it's more difficult to stay focused on the upcoming notes. If you learn to rewind almost to the exact place and not too far back every time, you'll save a lot of time and be able to keep your ears more focused.

20 Listen to this bar of some fast 16th notes from an organ solo.

Here's the first note:

21 If you learn to stop the machine accurately, it's easier to pick out the first three notes.

22 Then target the next two.

23 Then the next two.

24 Add two more.

25 Then the last two.

26 Here's the whole thing again.

Here are the notes.

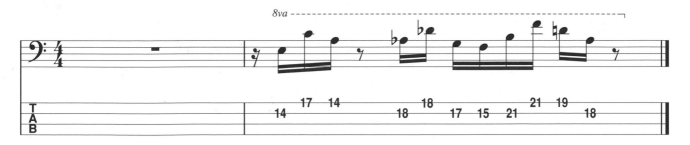

INTERVAL LEARNING

"My Bonnie Lies Over The Ocean"

Major 6th up, right?

Not exactly.

OK, you can use familiar tunes to remind yourself of the names of intervals, but you'll only find it useful on tests. It rarely has a real-world application. See if you can recognize this popular cartoon theme from the following example.

I rest my case.

Answer: ⅁ əuoʇsuᴉlℲ əɥ┴

61 BASS SOLO SYMPTOMS

Bass solos tend to suffer from common afflictions. The foremost is a lack of interesting intervals or shapes. There are a couple of reasons for this. First of all, the hardest thing to do on bass is to cross strings, especially ascending. This is why most bass solos include a lot of adjacent notes, small intervals, mostly steps and half steps because it's easier to only cross one string at a time. Another reason is that most improvisation is learned with chord/scale relationships. So, if the first thing you think of is the correct scale, then your scale ideas will also include this adjacent-note, close-together symptom.

Another bass solo symptom is including the root at the beginning or the end of an idea. This is a common malady that comes from the need to keep your place in the tune. If you want to create a sense of harmony that sounds above the music, no matter what register you play in, you need to avoid emphasising the root at the beginning and end of your ideas (see tip #3).

The solution for the interval problem is to simply start including larger intervals and more of them. They help create energy and broaden the spectrum of the ideas. One way to practice this is to force yourself to avoid half steps and whole steps in a solo. Another way to practice this is to just solo on non-adjacent strings: the A and the G, or the E and the D. It won't be easy, but it'll help you to start seeing a bigger picture.

The first solution to root-oriented soloing is "don't do that". Force yourself to avoid roots at critical points in your phrasing. Another thing that will help is memorizing the tune well enough that you don't have to guide yourself through it with the roots. Practicing with backing tracks or making sure that the keyboard or guitarist in the band comps will help as well.

62 BIGGER IS BETTER

When I first started playing a 5-string, I used a .125 and then a .128 for the B string. I found that these only gave me decent sounding notes up to the 7th fret. Any notes above that were pretty useless. The .135 I use now gives me useful notes up to and past the 12th fret. I recommend using at least a .130.

Here's what usually happens. A lighter gauge string will have less tension than a larger gauge string. The lighter gauge string is looser and has a tendency to buzz more. In order to compensate for this buzz, you raise the string height. This stops the buzzing but takes the string further away from the pickup, reducing its output so you have to play it harder. Playing it harder results in more buzzing, and you eventually run out of options. A larger B string has more tension so it's not as likely to buzz. This means you can keep your string height closer to the pickup like the rest of the strings. This proximity to the pickup keeps its output consistent with the other strings. Also, the larger size of the string means the pickup "sees" more and will have more output as well. This means you don't have to play the string harder (reducing the buzz factor) to get the same output.

63 NATURAL HARMONICS

A natural harmonic will occur when you divide a string in half and play it. For instance, located at the 12th fret is a "node". A node is a spot on a string that doesn't vibrate. If you touch the G string at the node on the 12th fret (don't fret it) with your left hand and play it, you'll hear the note one octave higher. Another node is at the 7th fret. This will produce a note an octave and a fifth up (D). At the 5th fret is a node that produces a note two octaves up. Between the 5th fret and the nut are many more nodes, but they don't correspond to any frets.

Natural harmonics are great for tuning up. All you need is to get one string in tune (usually the G string) and then you can use natural harmonics to tune up the rest of the strings. The node at the 7th fret of the G string produces a D that's an octave and a half up. The node at the 5th fret of the D string produces a D that's two octaves up. Since they're the same note, use the natural harmonic D from your G string to measure your natural harmonic D from the D string. Once they match, use the same pair of natural harmonics down a string to tune up the A string: D string, 7th fret and A string, 5th fret. Continue down once more and you're finished tuning a 4-string bass. Twice more for a 5-string.

Here's where the natural harmonics occur in the first 12 frets and the corresponding notes they produce:

(The notes are played on the G string from right to left to correspond to the fingerboard.)

64 FALSE HARMONICS

False harmonics are different from natural harmonics. Natural harmonics occur on open strings. Most people use them to tune up (tip #63). False harmonics involve the same technique but with a fretted note. Play the C on your G string, 5th fret. Now play it while touching the C an octave up (17th fret). That's a false harmonic. Now move your left hand up and play that C on the 17th fret. Exactly half the distance from there to the bridge is the spot to touch to get the false harmonic an octave up to sound for that note.

If you imagine a miniature fingerboard starting with the 24th fret, your right hand can imitate the fingering locations of your left hand on this miniature fingerboard, and all the notes will sound an octave higher. Two different techniques for playing false harmonics are found in tip #98.

Here's a C major scale played with false harmonics:

65 IMAGINARY 24TH FRET

This one is useful If you have a 21-fret neck and you want to use false harmonics (tip #64). Imagining the miniature fingerboard that starts above the 24th fret is more difficult without some kind of visual reference. Since there's no 24th fret, you can make one yourself. Use a piece of narrow 1/64" wide graphic tape, or cut a similar strip of colored (your choice) tape and place it on the body exactly underneath where the 24th fret would be. This is exactly 1/4th the length of the string. It's easy to find since it's a naturally occuring node of the string. For instance, play the G string while touching it at this point, and you'll hear a G two octaves up. Put the indicating tape directly under this spot. That's where the first fret of the imaginary miniature fingerboard begins.

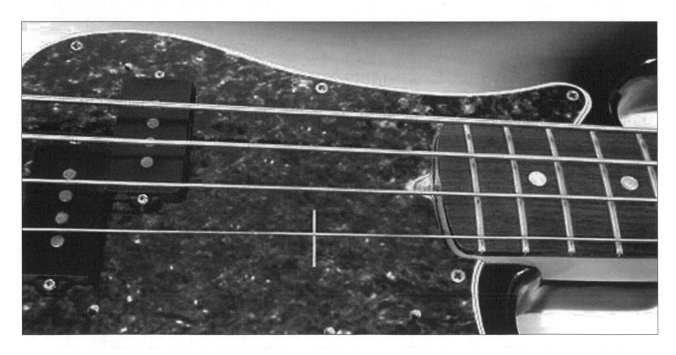

66 FALSE HARMONIC TRICK

This tip is the opposite of #65. Instead of your right hand closely imitating the notes you play in the left hand, the concept is to play lower on the fingerboard and don't imitate the fingering with your right hand at all. The best results come from notes within the first five frets. Don't worry about where you locate your finger or thumb for the node. Usually the best sounds come from a location over or close to the back pickup. The result is similar to the overtones of a distortion stomp box and can be a lot of fun.

Here's what it can sound like:

67 LEFT-HAND MUTING

Ever get a high-pitched ring even though you're sure you're damping with your left hand? It's probably because you've accidentally created a harmonic. Even though you're touching the string thinking it's damped, unless you touch it in two different places, odds are you're going to get a harmonic. For instance, if you play an open E and dampen it with your left hand resting at the 5th fret, that's where the two-octave harmonic will occur. You'll hear an E two octaves up. If you carefully use your 1st and your 4th finger to dampen the string, it'll be quiet. You can use all four fingers if you want, as long as you stay relaxed. Whatever works!

68 "JUMPING BASS" SYNDROME

There comes a time in every bassist's life when it's time to walk. All kinds of styles eventually need some form of four-notes-to-the-bar to get from point A to point B or to create some momentum. Since it puts more demands on your knowledge of the fingerboard, it usually leads to the dreaded "Jumping Bass" syndrome. Instead of smoothly connecting bass lines that weave their way through the harmony, the lines jump and flail awkwardly, sometimes at random, but usually coinciding with a new chord or key change.

The solution isn't pretty… It involves a dedicated effort to learn the fingerboard well enough so that new keys and chord changes won't interrupt the flow of the line. The first step is to develop more than one "look" at a chord. Bassists that exhibit this syndrome tend to chase chords around all over the neck relying on a single shape or "look" for each chord. Learning more than one way to view a chord will increase your options and help eliminate *linus interruptus* (clinical term for Jumping Bass). For example, learn to look at a V7 chord starting with the 2nd finger *and* the 4th finger. Or be able to see a "two" chord from your 4th finger and your first finger. Another way to help eliminate the "jumps" is to confine your hand to an area on the neck and work on connecting lines in that area. This approach usually demands an alternate "view" of some of the chords involved. With your help and participation, we here at the Jumpin' Bass Clinic hope to stamp out *linus interruptus* in our lifetime. Thank you for your support.

69 LIGHT GAUGE STRINGS

Light gauge strings make a bass easier to play, but they also introduce a couple of problems. Lighter strings have less tension, which creates an easier playing feel, but because there's less tension the string vibrates more freely and is more likely to buzz. Higher action will help reduce the buzz but starts to offset the easier-to-play benefit. Also, with smaller strings, the pickup "sees" less, so there's less output. Smaller strings bend easier so they need more attention to keep them in tune. Make sure you consider these aspects before you switch to a smaller set.

What about large gauges? Switching from a medium set to a large set also has its own set of problems. Mainly, the extra tension that a larger string provides can reduce its ability to sustain. Also, larger gauges may require larger slots filed into the nut so the strings will fit. There are all kinds of variations in alloys, core thickness versus wrap thickness, and string length according to the bass design, but the standard sizes for E-A-D-G (.105-.085-.065-.045) are generally what most basses are designed to use and will provide a good starting point.

70 CABLE INFOMERCIAL

Really, I'm not here to sell you a Monster Cable™, just to inform you that cables can make a difference. The cables available today are way better than what was available ten years ago. I used to solder my own cables using quality Mogami 4-conductor w/shield. I thought I was getting good results until I heard differently. If your bass is passive (it operates without a battery), then it is more subject to cable-ization (signal is affected by the cable) than if it's active—although you can hear the difference with an active bass as well.

71 WORKING OUT

If you're going to work out with weights or machines, opt for the machines. Free weights require more squeezing from your hands than weight machines. This leads to your fingers and all the muscles and tendons in your forearms getting stronger, but this strength comes at a price. The stronger your fingers get while working together doing the same thing (like squeezing the bar on free weights), the more you'll lose the flexibility and independence you need to maintain to play the bass. Weight machines are less hand-intensive but usually still give you the workout you're looking for.

72 MUSCLE MEMORY

Learning to play in tune on a fretless is accomplished in two steps: hand-eye coordination and then eventually muscle memory. Once you've reached the point where you're starting to rely on muscle memory, then it helps to keep the physical dimensions of your instrument from changing when you switch from fretless to fretted. If you're playing basses that are different, then this muscle memory won't be reinforced when you switch. Your intonation can suffer, and it'll take longer to achieve consistent intonation. Having identical fretless and fretted basses will help reinforce the muscle memory necessary to stay in tune.

73 ONE STRING AT A TIME

Removing all the strings at once releases all the tension on the neck from the strings. Since the truss rod serves to counter this tension, when the tension is removed, the truss rod ends up pulling the neck in the opposite direction into a back bow. Although it's not necessarily damaging, the more movement the neck undergoes, the less likely it will stay "settled" into that perfect balance between string tension and truss-rod tension. Changing one string at a time eliminates these drastic swings in tension for the neck and keeps it more stable.

74 ANOTHER FRETLESS DON'T

Although this one might be a no-brainer for a lot of you, it actually came up in a review of my fretless signature bass so here it is for the record. Fretless basses are not intended to be slapped, popped, thumbed, or whatever you want to call it—even the ones with a finished fingerboard. In a violent collision between metal and epoxy, metal and polyurethane, or especially metal and wood, the metal will always win. Even frets will eventually lose this contest and wear out. The lifespan of a fretless neck will be severly reduced by slapping; save it for the frets.

EAR IMPROV

Most students tell me that they can sing or whistle a better solo than they can actually play. That's because a lot of improvistation methods don't include the ear or the imagination in the learning process. Here's a simple exercise to get you to start including your imagination. It's based on the fact that you've been exposed to enough music in your lifetime that your imagination has already developed a way of responding musically to what your hear or play. All you need to do is leave some space, listen, and you can start to connect your imagination to the fingerboard. Improvisation involves the use of a musical vocabulary to express and develop ideas. Just like the study of the vocabulary in a new language, you have to initially limit your focus. The first goal is to learn how to develop shapes. That means we need to limit ourselves to a few simple rhythms, since rhythm *and* phrasing is too much to take on in the beginning. To get better access to your imagination, it's better not to have to worry about the chord changes, so we'll limit the progression to two chords, two bars each: Cm7 to Fm7.

Listen to the first idea I play, and pay attention to what your imagination wants to hear afterwards:

31

Odds are you probably imagined something like this:

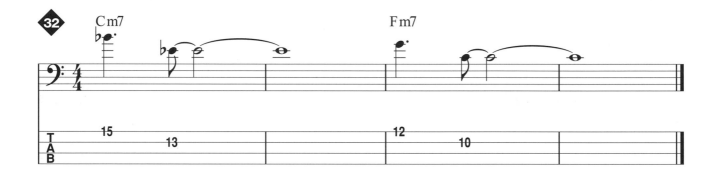

Here's an example of how this idea can be developed:

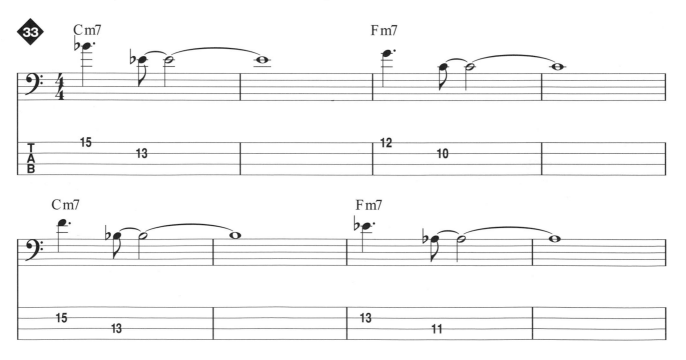

54

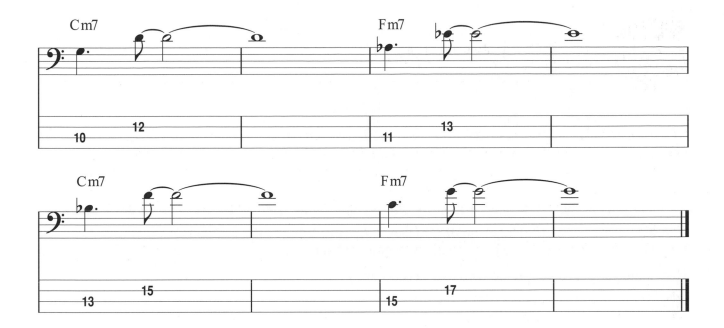

By playing and leaving space, your ear is given time to imagine and react. The more you practice this way, with the ear in mind, the more you can close the gap between the solos that happen when you sing or whistle and the ones you can actually perform.

Here's a few examples of some two-, three-, and four-note ideas to work with on this exercise.

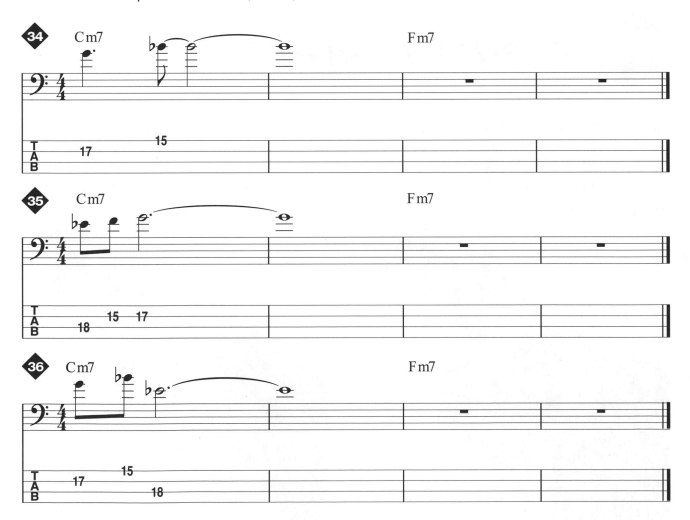

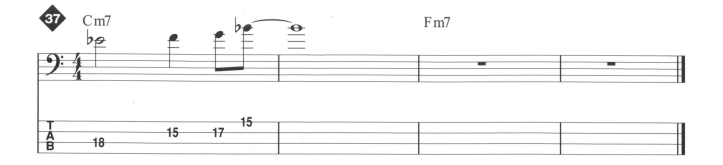

Remember to strictly imitate the rhythms so that you can concentrate on just developing the shapes.

Some people suggest singing along as you play to achieve similar results. I found it didn't work for me at all. My voice eventually just ended up following what my hands wanted to do.

Here's the same progression for you to practice with.

76 AVOID THE SALUTE

A common habit of less-experienced players is the left-hand salute. Individual fingers that are not busy fretting tend to stand at attention, pointing to the sky. This involuntary motion is actually a lot of work for the left hand, considering all the saluting-fretting back to saluting-fretting… over and over just to play a simple groove. It really can slow down any technique and speed you try to develop.

This exercise forces you to keep your non-fretting fingers in contact with the fingerboard.

The following sequence shows you the position your fingers should be in for each note:

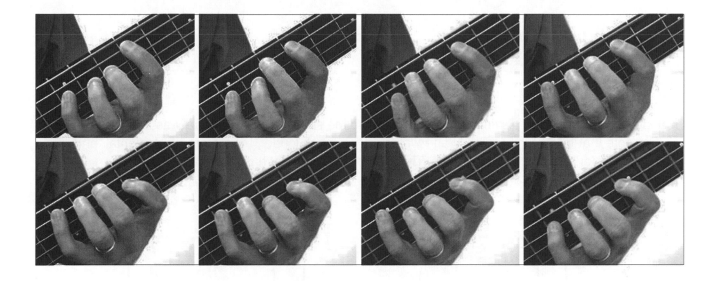

Make sure to keep your fingers relaxed. The eventual goal is to keep your fingers close to the neck when they're not fretting.

77 THE BENEFITS OF PLAYING SOFT

Gather around the campfire, kids… A long time ago, I used to play the bass very hard with my right hand. I had the usual symptoms: calluses, tendonitis, etc. I was having to shake my hand out sometimes in the middle of tunes in order to keep it loose enough to play. I started noticing the difference in tone that I got when I practiced through the same amp at home that I used on the gig. The sound was much fatter when I played soft than when I dug in and played hard. At first I thought it was just because there wasn't some drummer around bashing, making it hard to hear anything. Luckily there was a Physics for Musicians class that I had to take at North Texas State University. Of course, this is in no way supposed to be treated as scientific data, but here's my slightly educated guess at what goes on:

The more force you use to play a note on electric bass, the more the tone suffers. Playing hard will generate a big gnarly attack, but that just creates a bigger difference between the attack and the volume where the string wants to settle in and vibrate:

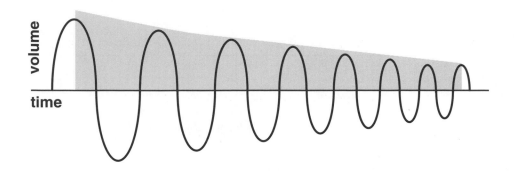

Note played hard…
creates louder attack…
but quicker decay.

Turning your amp up and playing softer will still make the speaker act as if there was a big attack, but the note that follows immediately afterwards will be much louder, have more fundamental, and sound bigger for a much longer duration. This is especially true for a fretless:

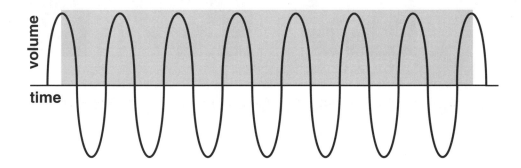

With amp turned up…
speaker reacts the same…
but the sound stays louder with more fundamental, lasts longer.

Besides having a big effect on tone, playing softer has several other benefits:

• Since your right hand doesn't have to work as hard, it can be more efficient and, well, faster.

• Since the strings aren't being struck as hard, they don't have as big of a vibration pattern, so you can lower the action, and this makes the bass easier to play.

• Once you lower the action, you get the strings closer to the pickup, and the pickup "sees" more string, and this will give you a fatter tone as well.

The most important benefit of playing softer is the headroom you leave yourself for dynamics. Dynamics, the different volumes you are able to play and even the differences in volume between individual notes, make for a much more musical impact and have a much stronger impact on the overall feel of the music.

78 DAMPENING SYSTEM

Whenever you play on your upper strings, you need to make sure that the lower ones don't ring sympathetically. There are two basic methods. The most common is to rest your thumb on the lower strings as you play on the upper strings. Another, less common technique is to use the 3rd and 4th fingers to dampen the two lower strings. Here's a look at both methods.

normal technique

alternate technique

If you use a 5- or 6-string bass, then you have to be careful with either technique and make sure that your lower strings are dampened. The tendency is to leave the B string undampened. You don't just have to play an upper B to get the open B to start ringing; any note will start it vibrating. Sometimes it's not that audible, but once you notice it (especially in a recording) it will quickly become annoying. Since I use the thumb approach, with a little more effort I can get my three lower strings covered. With the other method, the thumb, 3rd, and 4th finger remain in contact with the lower strings.

On a 5- or 6-string bass

79 THE PALM MUTE

In the last few years, I've found myself using muted notes more and more often. Instead of muting with my fingers, I use the side of my palm to control the sound and duration of the notes. Since I like to play music that develops and grows, starting out a section of music with a muted sound allows me to transition to a more full-sounding "fingers" tone later on, which helps the tone of the bass as well as the character of the music develop over time.

To achieve a muted sound, what you can do is place your palm just over the saddles on the bridge. You might need to file the bottom of the saddle screws down if they sit up too high, unless you enjoy the pain. I mostly use my thumb, index, and middle finger to play the notes. You can vary the amount of pitch versus "thump" you get out of the note by experimenting with the pressure and location of your palm on the saddles.

Once you locate your palm in the right position on the saddles, you can change the sound of the notes from very short and percussive to a long full sound by just varying the pressure from your palm. One of the advantages to muting with your palm is that the notes aren't as bright as regular notes and help you "stay out of the way" of other instruments when needed. Since the pitches aren't as defined as your regular notes, the activity of the bass lines works more like another percussion instrument.

Here's a bass line that uses palm muting:

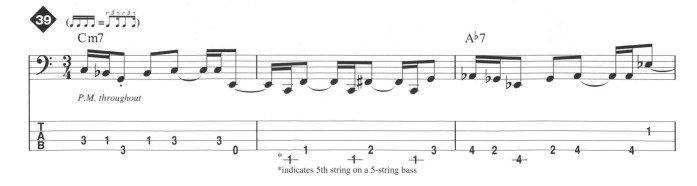

Here's the groove so you can try it yourself:

80 THE BARRE JOINT

The *barre* is a technique with the left hand where your finger frets two or more adjacent strings at a time. It's rare that you'll need to play more than two notes at a time, but the technique can speed up a lot of the ideas that occur normally on bass. The barre on bass produces a perfect fourth. A majority of grooves, lines, and ideas on bass involve fourths. Barring makes these 4ths much easier to play.

Although it's considered good technique to play with the tips of your fingers, the ability to barre or flatten out your fingers is a must for getting around the fingerboard. This exercise will give you the most control for barring. It involves pivoting on the tips of your fingers using the last knuckle in each finger. Position your fingers like this on the A string:

Keep the tips of your fingers on the A string and bend the last knuckle of each finger so that it frets the note on the same fret on the D string. In between the notes on the D string, flex your finger back out of the way and play an open D. Here are the notes:

Here's what it should look like when you play the upper notes:

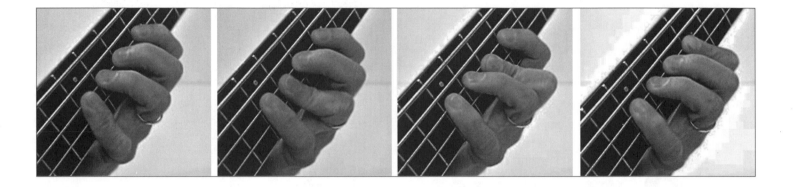

The last joint on each finger might not be flexible enough to do this right away. If you feel any pain or tension, stop. You can work on the flexibility without the bass. Place the tip of your finger on your thumb and work on flexing that last joint. Over a period of time, you should be able to loosen it up until it will begin to work with this exercise.

81 PINKY FLEX

I've seen a tendency for people to lock the joints of the little finger while fretting. While this sometimes helps when you're playing on the lower strings, it can become a liability when you play on upper strings. A straightened little finger forces the rest of the hand away from the neck and prevents the other fingers from being immediately available to play notes.

A simple technique will help you to learn to keep your little finger bent:

Put the palm of your hand in contact with the neck, and play a D major scale from the D on the E string to the D on the D string. Keep your palm in contact with the side of the neck for all the notes. Since it's impossible to keep your little finger bent while playing on the D string, you can start to get a feel for how to keep it flexible.

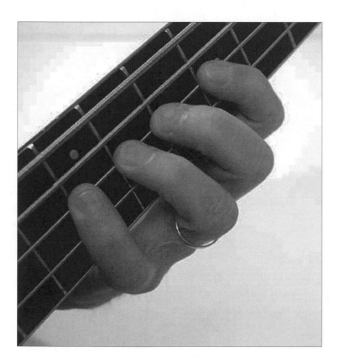

⟨82⟩ RIGHT-HAND NOTE DAMPENING

I discovered early on that dampening with the right hand has lots of advantages. At first I was concerned with eliminating the buzz that happens when you dampen with the left hand. By eliminating the buzz, italso makes it easier to turn up and play softer (tip #77). Of course, you turn up and play softer while dampening with the left hand, but you end up turning up the buzz as well. Another benefit of right-hand dampening is that the act of dampening places a finger on a string ready to go. So you're immediately prepared to play the next note without any effort. If you incorporate a rest stroke (landing on the next string on the follow-through), you also end up with a finger on a string ready to go.

Here's an exercise to get you started with right-hand dampening. This one can be done with regular two-finger technique or with my three-finger technique.

- Two-finger version:

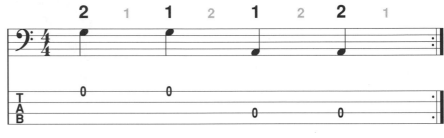

- Three-finger version:

1. The G's and A's are open strings. Completely remove your left hand from the neck.

2. The bold numbers indicate which finger plays; the gray numbers indicate which finger dampens.

3. Go slow… I mean really slow. ♩ = 30… that's right, 30.

4. If you're comfortable with the sequence of notes and all your fingers are doing what they should, do not try to go faster. Stay at the same tempo and play short notes. Since you're stopping the note with the finger that's going to play next, you're preparing yourself to play fast. Staying at a slow tempo and playing short notes gives you plenty of time to relax in between notes. Teach yourself to relax, and playing fast will always be easier.

83 RECORD YOUR PRACTICING

This is especially valuable if you're working on improvisation. You'll find yourself hearing things that you don't normally notice when you're busy thinking about changes and scales and fingerings, etc. Improvisation involves learning a vocabulary so that you can express yourself. Recording your practicing can help you become more familiar with your own vocabulary and help you edit it in order to be more effective. Of course, you're liable to decide "I'll never play that lick again," but you might also be surprised at the cool ideas that go undeveloped or unexplored, and you can go back and start including them in your vocabulary.

84 THE EXTRA MILE

Occasionally a drastic shift from one register to the other is required. However difficult it might seem to go from, for instance, notes above the 12th fret to notes in the first five frets, you can make it seem easier. It involves tricking your brain. Say you had to quickly go from a B♭ on the G string, 15th fret to a G on the E string, 3rd fret. Try adding an extra non-musical step to the process, like touching the headstock in between. Once you add that extra step and work it up to a pretty good speed, eliminating the extra step makes the shift a piece of cake.

85 LOOK AT THE NECK

The bass fingerboard is symmetric. When you learn a shape like a major third (the physical distance is a string and a fret), you can play that shape and expect to hear a major third anywhere you go on the fingerboard, as long as you have a string and a fret available. Other instrumentalists aren't so lucky. A keyboard has four different ways of playing a major third (white note to a white note, white note to a black note, black note to a white note, black note to a black note.) Woodwinds have even more combinations of fingerings to achieve a major third.

Looking at the neck will help you to start understanding this symmetry and incorporating it into how you look at harmony.

86 LOOK AT YOUR RIGHT HAND

I wish I had a dollar for every time I've seen this one. Most students, if given an exercise for the right hand, will invariably begin to look up into outer space, or at least the far wall or ceiling. It's especially true if the right-hand exercise is particulary challenging—there's the automatic gaze toward the skies.

Look at your right hand! These are fine, difficult-to-master motor skills that need your undivided attention. The sooner your start looking at your right hand, the sooner you'll be able to spot problems and find solutions.

One reason that the right hand suffers from neglect is that the left hand and the study of harmony on the fingerboard is usually a very slow process, sometimes taking years to accomplish. During that time, the technical challenges for the right hand happen very gradually, so it's able to keep up with the pace of learning with little or no extra attention. Then, after a period of years, you end up with a right hand technique that you hope will serve you well as you go on to more difficult challenges. What happens a lot is that bad technique habits get ingrained early on and don't become obvious until the left hand finally starts challenging the right hand years later.

87 EAR TRAINING EXERCISE

I've always maintained that your ear is the most valuable asset you have as a musician. Here's a good way to make sure it stays sharp. Make your own ear-training imitation exercise, or practice with a friend.

Decide on an area of the neck or a key within a specific place on the neck. Pick a starting note. Play anything from two- to four-note ideas in that area of the neck. If you're making a recording, leave time for an answer or assume that you'll hit the pause button. Begin each succesive idea with the last note of the previous idea. For instance, if you play a C to a G, then follow that with an idea from G.

If you're working with someone else, you can quickly start to narrow down what you need to work on and see improvement. Working with your own recording will get the same results but may be a little slower. Here's a couple to get you started.

This one starts and ends with the C (2nd finger) on the E string. All the notes are from the C major scale (diatonic).

This one starts and ends with the same C but the notes are chromatic, though still within the same (five-fret) area.

PC BOARD SPACERS

Before I got the opportunity to design my signature bass, I was looking for a way to add tension to the lower strings (B and E) without resorting to a 35" scale or obnoxiously big string gauges. A fairly easy way to tighten up the B and the E is with PC board spacers. These little 1/4" spacers are fairly easy to find at electronic stores. Slip them over the strings before you insert the strings through the bridge. The length of spacer is sometimes limited by the cloth wrap at the other end of the string. The wrap could contact or rest on the nut if you try to extend the string too far in the other direction. A half an inch is usually safe and will make a noticeable difference in tension.

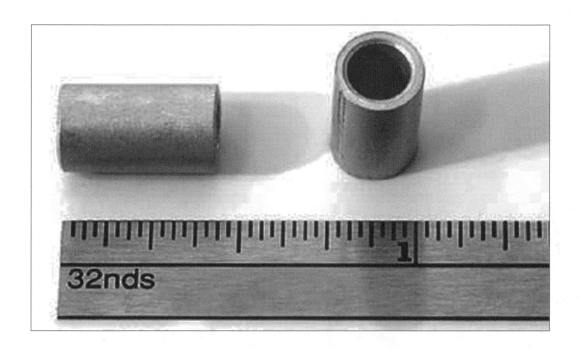

89 CHORD TONES THRU CHANGES

This is a good way to get a handle on how to move ideas containing chord tones through changes. Just play whole notes through a progression and try to move the notes stepwise through the changes. This will teach you good "voice leading," which can help you resolve your ideas through changes better.

Try it with this progression: Em7–A7–Dm7–G7.

Here are some examples:

47 Here's the progression so you can work on it yourself.

90 STUDIO TRACKING SETUP

Even the finest headphones won't give you the real sensation of playing bass like you can get in front of an amp. We're used to having our torso vibrated to "feel" those lows. There's no way to get that sensation from headphones. The first thing I discovered that helped was to never try to track bass in the same room with the drums (that's why they call it the drum room). If the studio is constructed in the traditional way, then large monitors are probably built into an overhang or ledge facing the mixing board. If you can stand and record underneath one of these speakers, you'll be standing in a "bass trap" and will be able to hear and feel the low end much better. Finally, there's no substitute for the real thing. All it takes is a small bass system with a 10" or a couple of 10's positioned up high, immediately behind you to get that torso-thumping live feel. The proximity of the speakers keeps you from having to turn them up very much at all, and you get the added benefit of being able to hear yourself better without always asking to be turned up in the headphone mix.

91 SECONDARY DOMINANTS

A lot of chord changes happen in one key. You don't have to be Stravinsky to realize that this gets boring rather quickly. By inserting secondary dominants into chord changes, composers can add interest while still using chord changes that sound like they belong together. Here's how you can take advantage of secondary dominants as a bass soloist:

A dominant chord is built from the root of the 5th of a key. It gets its name from the "dominant resolution" that takes place when you go from the V chord to the I chord in a key.

A dominant chord is called secondary if it doesn't normally occur as a dominant in a key. For instance, the progression Cmaj7–Am7–Dm7–G7 is all in the key of C. The only dominant chord is the G7, and it occurs naturally in the key of C. If we change the Am7 to an A7, it becomes a secondary dominant. It temporarily implies the V chord in the key of D. This still sounds like it belongs to the progression because of the "pull" of the secondary dominant chord. The harmony is pointed towards the Dm7 and then immediately returns back to the key of C with the other changes.

This information becomes useful when you're improvising and want to create more interest by substituting these kinds of secondary dominants. Here's an example of the chord tones that you should target to imply the secondary dominants. In almost every case, the chord tone that needs playing is the third.

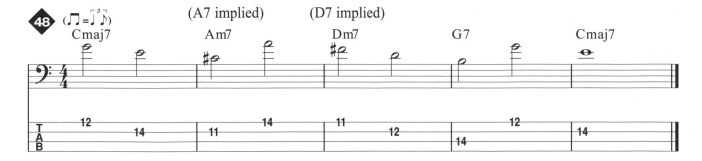

When you start to solo with these chord tones in mind, you won't play the target notes so long, but just use them as part of your ideas:

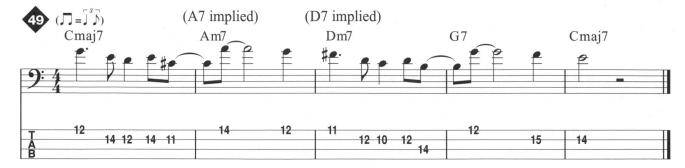

Here's another example:

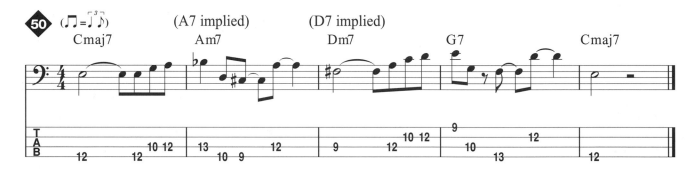

Here's the progression for you to practice with.

92 STATIC HARMONY FIX

If you're playing over seemingly endless bars of Dm7, you can create interest by substituting some root movement that implies harmonic motion. These strategically placed notes that imply movement can help everyone hear where they are in the progression (for instance, in 24 bars of Dm7) and solidify the band's phrasing. As an example, at the end of a four-bar phrase, if you imply a II–V in the last bar, it helps make the harmony sound like it's getting a new start at the beginning of the next eight-bar section. Listen to these first two examples.

The first one is fine but doesn't imply any movement:

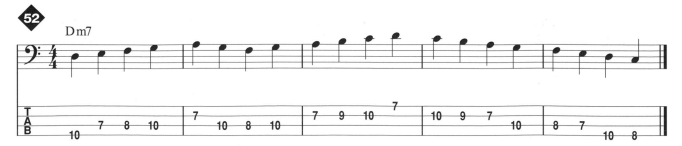

The second one implies a ii-V in the 4th bar:

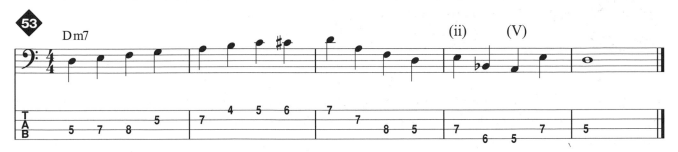

You can use this approach a couple of other ways. For instance, you could imply just a V chord in the last bar:

Or you could use the last two bars to imply the ii–V progression.

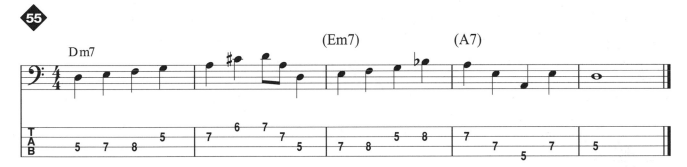

Or even a III–IV–II–V in the last two bars.

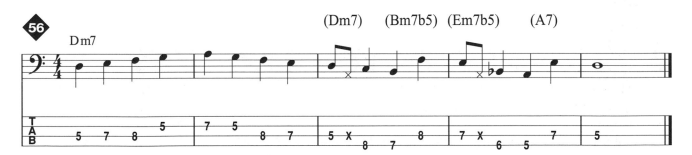

Once you get comfortable with the concept, you'll be able to choose when to use this approach to the greatest effect. Sometimes, it's better not to chop the music up into little sections. That way you're able to use it only when it's needed.

Here's a groove you can practice these lines with.

93 THE TRITONE SUB

No, it's not the latest nuclear offering from the Navy. It's a way to create more interesting harmony movement, and it's possible to do on the bass by itself. Here's how the tritone sub works:

Take an innocent G7 chord moving to C. The most important notes of any chord are the 3rd and the 7th—in this case, B and F. A tritone gets its name from a distance of three whole tones. It's the same as an augmented 4th or diminished 5th. A tritone from G is D♭. Combine that D♭ with the B and the F and you get D♭7. From G7 to C, the chord tones B and F resolve smoothly to C and E. The same resolution happens to those two notes when you go from D♭7 to C. The added benefit is the more interesting movement from D♭ to C in the bass.

Here's G7 to C with the regular G to C root movement:

Here's G7 to C with the tritone sub root movement D♭ to C:

Here's G7 to C with no roots so you can try it either way:

The 5th of any chord is the least crucial to the chord (except when it's altered) and can be easily left out of chord voicings without any consequences. When keyboard and guitar players use these kinds of voicings, it's possible for you to create your own tritone sub just by changing the bass notes.

Make sure that you're aware of how they're treating the dominant chord, though. It's common for them to spice up the harmony and use altered (♯5 and ♯9) voicings to create interest as well. These altered chord tones are not interchangeable like the 3rds and 7ths. The altered chord tones of G7, D♯ and A♯, become the plain vanilla 9th and 13th of D♭. Although both you and the harmony instrument are trying to make things more interesting, simultaneous substitutions won't get the best results.

94 CHORD TONE PROXIMITY

This little bit of trivia could change the way you look at the fingerboard: You're never more than a whole step from a chord tone. This is actually true of any instrument. Take a G7. If you take into account all the G's, B's, D's, and F's available, you can't find a note that's more than a whole step from any of these notes. Does your playing take full advantage of this fact?

Didn't think so…

95 BOOMY ROOM MIX

How many soundchecks have ended with the phrase "It'll sound better once the place fills up?" If you find yourself trying to soundcheck in an empty concert hall with the low freqencies just bouncing all over the place and dominating the sound, try this—roll off the frequencies from about 50Hz and below out of the PA—then at least you can finish your soundcheck. With any luck, you'll sell out the venue, fill up the hall, and all those warm bodies will soak up all that low end that was dominating the sound before. At that point, it'll be necessary to put the low end back in the PA, and everyone will be happy.

96 THE 2X4 SOLUTION

The most important part of slap technique is the right hand. Great grooves depend on the accuracy and feel you develop in your right hand. Right-hand slap technique is very similar to the left hand of a traditional-grip drummer. The wrist rotates as the two large bones in the forearm move back and forth. Instead of practicing with the left hand and worrying about notes, just work on developing this motion. That's where the 2x4 comes in. Since they're made of light pine, they're very resonant and the contact points for your thumb and fingers are very audible. Since slap technique is basically a percussive device, treat it like one. Slap on the 2x4 as if it's a percussion instrument. You'll find that you'll challenge your hands into executing a lot more complex and interesting rhythms than if you were on your bass worrying about notes. Once these grooves and rhythms become natural, your right hand can easily adapt to playing the same rhythmic ideas on the bass.

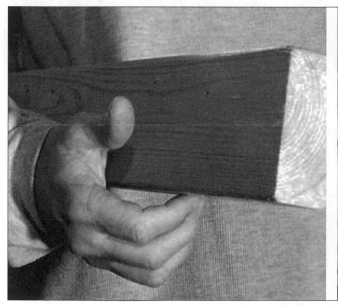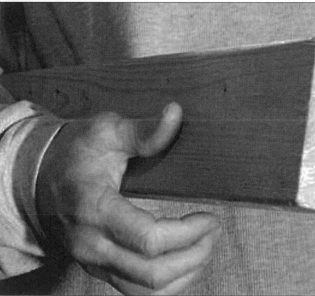

97 PASSIVE QUIRK

If you have a passive bass (no battery), realize that when you turn down the volume, you're also changing the EQ and turning down the highs. The output from a passive bass is called a high-impedence signal. When the resistance from turning down the volume loads the signal, the highs start to disappear. It's better to run the knobs on a passive bass all the way up so that you send the full-range signal to the amp. That way, you won't end up trying to put highs back into the signal that are taken out by reducing the volume at the bass.

98 FALSE HARMONIC TECHNIQUE

The standard way to play false harmonics is to contact the node with your thumb and strike the string with your first or second fingers.

Another way to play false harmonics is to use your first finger to contact the node and strike the string with your little finger. Since you're striking the string further from the node, it'll have more fundamental and sound fatter.

99 DIMINISHED CHORD IMPROV

Diminished chords got you down? Try this approach to get your ideas past the "diminished scale and arpeggio" approach. The notes of a B°7 chord are B, D, F, and A♭. Those are the same chord tones as G7♭9. Whenever you see a diminished chord, think of a 7♭9 chord down a major third and you'll end up playing more interesting ideas than the symmetrical diminished scales and arpeggios. You can also think down a half step for a 7♭9 chord. For the B°7, a B♭7♭9 will work just as well.

Try improvising over these changes and use the substitutions (grey) for the diminished changes.

Here are the chord tones you should emphasize:

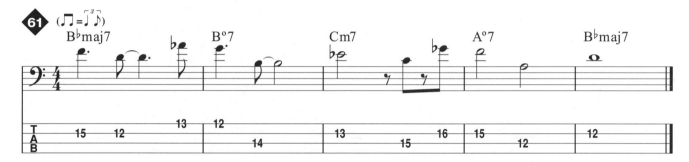

Here's a solo that uses those chord tones:

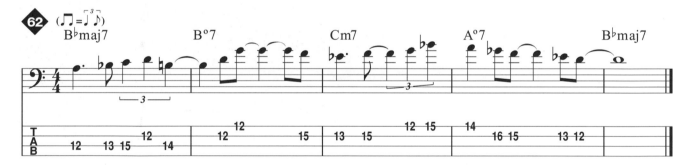

Here's another solo example:

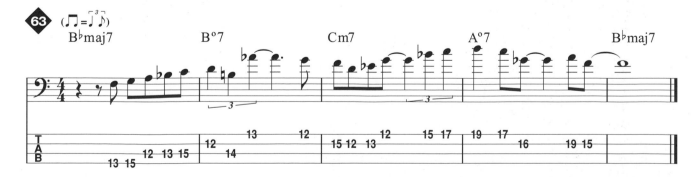

Here's the progression for you to practice with.

100 CLASSICAL POSTURE

A lot of our practicing is done sitting down. Although basses were designed to rest on your leg, playing this way can actually make your technique suffer. Notice where the bass sits in relation to your body when you're seated. Now, with the strap on of course, stand up but keep the bass where it was when you were sitting. Not very natural, is it? This can to lead to problems if you do all your practicing seated and your gigs standing up, especially if you're working on specific right-hand techniques.

You could stand up and practice, but an easier solution is to adopt a classical guitar posture. Rest the bass on your left leg, and it'll be resting much closer, almost exactly where it does when you stand.

101 APPENDAGE TIME

In order to develop an internal clock you can trust, it helps to start with an external one. Always keep the pulse with something—your foot, heel, hand, leg, whatever. You need a consistent pulse over which you can start imagining rhythms when you play. A common sight is a player tapping away with his/her foot until a different rhythm comes up and immediately the foot starts to try to follow the right hand. You need to develop some independence so that you can internalize the pulse and hear your ideas over it. Drummers are the best at this task, sometimes playing four different rhythms, one on each limb.

BASS BUILDERS
S E R I E S

A series of technique book/audio packages created for the purposeful building and development of your chops. Each volume is written by an expert in that particular technique. And with the inclusion of a CD, the added dimension of hearing exactly how to play particular grooves and techniques makes this truly like a private lesson. Books include notes and tab.

Bass Fitness—An Exercising Handbook
by Josquin des Pres
200 exercises designed to help increase your speed, improve your dexterity, develop accuracy and promote finger independence. Recommended by world-acclaimed bass players, music schools and music magazines!
00660177 Book Only..$7.95

Bass Improvisation— The Complete Guide to Soloing
by Ed Friedland
CD includes over 50 tracks for demonstration and play-along. The book works for electric or acoustic bass and covers: modes, harmonic minor, melodic minor, blues, pentatonics, diminished, whole tone, Lydian b7, and other important scales; phrasing, chord/scale concepts, melodic development, using your ear; and much more.
00695164 Book/CD Pack $17.95

Building Walking Bass Lines
by Ed Friedland
A walking bass line is the most common approach to jazz bass playing, but it is also used in rock music, blues, rockabilly, R&B, gospel, latin, country and many other types of music. The specific goal of this book is to familiarize players with the techniques used to build walking bass lines and to make them aware of how the process works. Through the use of 90-minutes' worth of recorded rhythm tracks, players will have the opportunity to put the new learning directly into action.
00695008 Book/CD Pack $17.95

Expanding Walking Bass Lines
by Ed Friedland
A follow-up to *Building Walking Bass Lines*, this book approaches more advanced walking concepts, including model mapping, the two-feel, several "must know changes," and other important jazz bass lessons.
00695026 Book/CD Pack $19.95

Fingerboard Harmony For Bass
A Linear Approach For 4-, 5- and 6-String Bass
by Gary Willis
Learn the theory and geometry of the bass fingerboard from one of today's leading players and instructors. The CD features Gary Willis demonstrating 99 examples and exercises. This comprehensive book covers hand positions, key centers, the linear approach, and much more.
00695043 Book/CD Pack $17.95

Funk Bass
by Jon Liebman
Critically acclaimed as the best single source for the techniques used to play funk and slap-style bass! Includes a foreword by John Patitucci and is endorsed by Rich Appleman of the Berklee College Of Music, Will Lee, Mark Egan, Stuart Hamm and many others! Features several photos and a special section on equipment and effects. A book for everyone – from beginners to advanced players! Includes a 58-minute audio accompaniment.
00699348 Book/CD Pack $17.95

Funk/Fusion Bass
by Jon Liebman
This follow-up to *Funk Bass* studies the techniques and grooves of today's top funk/fusion bass players. It includes sections on mastering the two-finger technique, string crossing, style elements, establishing a groove, building a funk/fusion soloing vocabulary, and a CD with over 90 tracks to jam along with. Features a foreword written by Earth, Wind And Fire bassist Verdine White.
00696553 Book/CD Pack $19.95

Jazz Bass
by Ed Friedland
This book/CD pack features over 50 examples covering walking bass, the two feel, 3/4 time, Latin, and ballads. It covers soloing, performance protocol, and includes seven complete tunes.
00695084 Book/CD Pack $17.95

The Lost Art of Country Bass
An Inside Look at Country Bass for Electric and Upright Players
by Keith Rosiér
endorsed by Leland Sklar and Glenn Worf
This book/CD pack teaches classic and modern bass lines in the style of Hank Williams, Lefty Frizzel, Marty Stuart, David Ball, and others. You'll learn: what gear the pros use; how to be a studio bassist; how to read music with the Nashville Numbering System; and more. The CD includes 33 songs with full band backing. In standard notation and tab.
00695107 Book/CD Pack $17.95

Muted Grooves
by Josquin des Pres
Develop the string muting, string raking, and right-hand techniques used by the greatest legends of bass with this comprehensive exercise book. It includes over 100 practical exercises with audio accompaniments for each.
00696555 Book/CD Pack $16.95

Simplified Sight-Reading for Bass
From the Fundamentals to the Entire Fingerboard
by Josquin des Pres
This book/CD pack helps bass players expand their reading skills. Beneficial for beginners through advanced players, this pack covers rhythms, notes, intervals, accidentals, and key signatures, as well as common bass patterns in blues, R&B, funk, rock, and more. The CD includes 97 demo tracks!
00695085 Book/CD Pack $17.95

Slap Bass Essentials
by Josquin des Pres and Bunny Brunel
This book/audio pack includes over 140 essential patterns and exercises covering every aspect of slap bass, written by two of today's hottest bass players Josquin des Pres and Bunny Brumell.
00696563 Book/CD Pack $16.95

FOR MORE INFORMATION, SEE YOUR LOCAL MUSIC DEALER, OR WRITE TO:

HAL•LEONARD®
CORPORATION
7777 W. BLUEMOUND RD. P.O. BOX 13819 MILWAUKEE, WI 53213
http://www.halleonard.com